If you sense that you have  k
will help you to look at yo It
will help you notice the t ou
can avoid them. And it es
when they knock so that you c... er
before has this important information been available in a form
that is so easy to understand and apply.

—Farrell Silverberg, PhD

Praise For Dr. Farrell Silverberg's *Make the Leap*

"We all need intelligent, practical help to get through our days—a lesson or an insight. Dr. Silverberg's book is deceptively simple in its language. Within all the crystal-clear analysis and advice is a deep sense of the invisible stories that affect our daily lives. This book can help you see the patterns that hold you back and ways of dealing with them effectively. Dr. Silverberg has transformed psycho-analysis into plain language and useful strategies."

—Thomas Moore, author of
Care of the Soul and *Dark Nights of the Soul*

"Remaining open to new experiences is one of life's greatest challenges. Ruts get deeper, and they become difficult to escape. Dr. Farrell Silverberg offers practical, no-nonsense escape routes for anyone who feels chained to boring, deadening routines—and who hasn't? If life has lost its zip, read this book."

—Larry Dossey, MD, author of
The Extraordinary Healing Power of Ordinary Things,
Reinventing Medicine, and *Healing Words*

"So much of our lives' energy is devoted to repeating the same patterns, maintaining the same ideas, and clutching on to what we believe is true. Farrell Silverberg, in this elegant and clear-minded work, shows us how to understand these patterns and reclaim the sense of wonder we once had as children. His understanding of what it means to be human has great depth and his guidance is accessible and clear. What a winning combination!"

—Daniel Gottlieb, PhD, family therapist,
Philadelphia Inquirer columnist,
host of WHYY's *Voices in the Family*

FARRELL SILVERBERG, PhD, is a training and supervising psychoanalyst at the Philadelphia School of Psychoanalysis and the Institute for Modern Psychoanalysis in New York City. The author of many articles on psychoanalysis, psychotherapy, and East-West psychology, he has been in private practice since 1984 in Philadelphia, where he lives.

Make

the Leap

Make
the Leap

A PRACTICAL GUIDE TO BREAKING THE
PATTERNS THAT HOLD YOU BACK

FARRELL SILVERBERG, PhD

Marlowe & Company
New York

MAKE THE LEAP:
A Practical Guide to Breaking the Patterns that Hold You Back
Copyright © 2005 by Farrell Silverberg

AVALON
publishing group incorporated

Published by
Marlowe & Company
An Imprint of Avalon Publishing Group Incorporated
245 West 17th Street • 11th Floor
New York, NY 10011-5300

Library of Congress Cataloging-in-Publication Data

Silverberg, Farrell.
    Make the leap : a practical guide to breaking the patterns that hold you back / Farrell Silverberg.
        p. cm.
    ISBN 1-56924-418-9 (pbk.)
        1. Change (Psychology) 2. Self-actualization (Psychology) I. Title.

    BF637.C4S55 2005
    158.1—dc22

                                                          2005007058

9 8 7 6 5 4 3 2 1

Book Design by Maria E. Torres

Printed in Canada

Dedicated to those *"who taught me this art . . ."*

—from the Hippocratic Oath, 4th century BCE

Our aspirations are our possibilities.

—Robert Browning

CONTENTS

Make
the Leap

PART ONE

The Pattern Problem & Solution

*I dreamed a thousand new paths . . .
I woke and walked my old one.*

—Chinese proverb

Freeing Your Potential

DO YOU FEEL, deep down, that you have the potential to live a better life than you are living now? And do you feel that you are not quite on the right track, or not quite moving at the right speed, to get to that better life? Or do you care about someone who fits this description? If so, this book is for you.

These days, if you feel you are not living the life you are meant to be living, odds are that you will be diagnosed with some condition. Maybe you'll be told you're a member of a group of people who need pills to help them adjust to life as it is. If that's really true, that's fine. But if not, it's a shame. It's a shame because, if you don't listen to your inner voice telling you that you should be living a better life, you will never have a chance to fulfill your full potential.

Listen to Your Inner Voice

What is that inner voice? It is a deep-down feeling that there should be something more, a sense there is something better waiting for you, if only you could find the path or energy to get to it.

People will say, "Oh, you poor dear, you are just down and you need to find a way to be happy." You'll be told you have to "adjust your attitude" and learn to enjoy living the life you know is not right for you.

However, if you have a nagging feeling that you are not living the right life or that you are not moving in the right direction, maybe your inner voice is telling you there *is* more promise in your life than you are fulfilling. Are areas in your life "less than" you believe they should be? Do you keep hitting a "glass ceiling" at work? Are your relationships not quite right? Maybe there is untapped potential inside of you. Maybe your hidden patterns are holding you back.

The difference between a successful person and an unsuccessful person is pretty simple. The successful person is achieving his or her goals, and the unsuccessful person is not. Have you ever been mystified trying to understand why you are not achieving your goals while a friend or colleague with seemingly equal potential is moving ahead with greater success? We usually can't figure it out and tend to attribute the difference to fate:

"Oh, she was just luckier than me." "Well, he had a better

upbringing than me." "She got a break that I didn't get." "He was just in the right place at the right time."

Even if others had more luck, or a better upbringing, or got help, or were in the right place at the right time, there is one particular ability that defines the difference between moving toward your goals and getting off track. That key factor is the ability to notice and take advantage of moments when opportunity is knocking. The key is knowing where, when, and how to make the leap.

You may have all the potential in the world, but if you are blind to noticing when the right path is directly in front of you or don't know what to do about it when you see it, you are going to underachieve in love, work, and life. Why? It is simply because you will miss chances to move ahead.

Chutes and Ladders

There is a child's board game called Chutes and Ladders, in which players take turns going around a track in an attempt to get to the finish line first. The chutes take you off track and backslide you to an earlier point from which you have to start over. The ladders are opportunities to move ahead and climb more quickly toward the goal.

Life is like a giant game of Chutes and Ladders. There are always traps that can cause you to backslide and start over. But there are also opportunities of which you can take advantage to move quickly and directly toward your goals.

Just like in the child's game, the opportunities in life come up often, but these opportunities only exist for a moment and then disappear as you move on.

The difference between people who are moving directly toward achieving their goals and those who are off course comes down to their ability to notice the chutes and ladders of life.

If you don't notice an opportunity to jump a level closer to your goals, you may never get there. If you don't notice when a trap is coming, and you don't foresee that taking a certain direction leads you to repeat a series of steps all over again, you spend a lot of time and energy going around in circles. It's a vicious cycle: when you miss chances to move ahead, your usual patterns continue; and when your usual patterns continue, you miss chances to move ahead.

The purpose of this book is to help you to better notice and take advantage of the chutes and ladders of life, to jump at the moments in which to seize an opportunity to climb, and to navigate past those moments in which you could slip so that you are not led around in circles.

Become Fit to Succeed

There are naturally successful people out there. You see them and read about them. Naturally successful people have potential, and in addition, they have a natural ability to notice the chutes and ladders. Naturally successful people avoid the detours and take advantage of the opportunities. That means that they can intuitively recognize pitfalls and shortcuts, and can intuitively figure out what to do about them. This is the formula for maximal fulfillment and achievement.

On the other hand, there are naturally unsuccessful people. They have the same potential as the naturally successful people. But instead of a natural ability to intuit life's opportunities and pitfalls, naturally unsuccessful people can't tell when these moments are upon them. Or, if they can intuit these moments, they are unable to make a quick enough decision about how to proceed, and might regret their indecisiveness later. This results in a life of underfulfillment and underachievement relative to their potential—a life with less happiness and less success than they deserve.

According to the famous scientist and father of the theory of evolution, Charles Darwin, the question of which creatures survive and which become extinct is decided by the "survival of the fittest": those who are naturally successful are most likely to survive and the rest will fall behind.

However, Darwin was wrong when it comes to people. This is because people *can* learn new things. There is a way for a naturally unsuccessful person to become a successful person. This may require going through an awkward in-between stage first. While learning a better approach to your life, like anyone learning a new skill, new sport, or new language, you might have to put extra thought and effort into working at it. Eventually someone who practices the correct way of being successful can learn how to be successful consistently and effortlessly.

Remember what it was like when you first learned how to drive? How unnatural it all was? Now it is probably a very routine activity. How did it become natural? You practiced the correct way to do it over and over again.

How come you learned to drive but you didn't learn how to be successful and fulfill your potential in life, work, and love? Probably because, having never driven before, no old patterns interfered with your success.

In learning our basic approach to life—in learning the how to navigate the chutes and ladders of life—each of us developed certain characteristic patterns. Often those patterns get in the way. They cloud our vision. They lure us down the chutes that cause us to backslide or run us around in circles. Patterns can cause you to become so caught up in your circles that you don't even see the shortcuts and ladders when they momentarily appear—so you pass by chances and ignore warnings.

It's Not All-or-Nothing

Now, this is not an all-or-nothing situation. There's an old saying, "Lucky at cards, unlucky in love." This means that sometimes you are fortunate and have your natural instinct to succeed in one area of life, but lack it in another. For instance, if you are a success in your career but your love life is empty or troubling, it might mean that no patterns are clouding your career judgments, but patterns are negatively affecting your love life.

Many people with potential to live better lives simply cannot tell when life is offering them a shortcut and when life is placing a detour in their paths. And, since this is not an all-or-nothing situation, others may have some ability to tell the difference, but can't do it consistently, while still other people have some ability to tell the difference but can't do it fast enough. They realize what they should have done just after the opportunity has passed.

If patterns are the culprit, why don't you notice them? The tricky thing about patterns is that you can get so accustomed to them that you don't even notice their presence. Your patterns might be so ingrained that they happen automatically (without being called to your attention) no matter how many missed opportunities or setbacks they cause.

You can't get out-of-the-box solutions if you are still inside the box, and you can't even try to get out of the box if you don't know you are inside it. This book will help you become aware of the patterns as they occur.

By reading this book you can learn to recognize what makes the difference between moving ahead and falling behind. You can learn how to uncover the moments of opportunity and weed out the traps. You can learn a method that shows you what to do to live a more successful and fulfilled life. You may want to learn this system to improve your entire life, or possibly you will want to learn it to improve one particularly clouded area of your life in which you feel your potential is not being met.

Why don't more people know about their patterns and the method to break them? The tools to help people fulfill their inner potential, to remove unproductive patterns and replace them with successful approaches, haven't been around very long. Understanding and overcoming patterns is a relatively young science, dating back only a hundred years, compared to other areas of medicine, such as surgery, that date back thousands of years.

The methods for helping people make this fundamental change on the intuitive level, a change in the unconscious mind, were invented by Sigmund Freud. But, as you have probably heard, Freud and his followers made their theories so terribly dense, quirky, and complicated, that they were either dismissed as blarney or else they could only be used by professional psychoanalysts. That is—until now.

Psychoanalysis Made Simple

Let's forget all the theories, sexual complexes, and jargon.

Let's not worry about fancy names in some scholarly language for every little habit. Instead, let's get down to the essentials of human nature and the practicalities of real life so you can become equipped with the knowledge you'll need to change your patterns. From years of studying, practicing, and teaching psychoanalysis, I came to the conclusion that the psychoanalytic theory about patterns can be summed up in the following six basic premises:

1. *All of us have patterns inside of us.*

2. *Some of our patterns help us in life, and others prevent us from reaching our goals.*

3. *Our patterns live in our "unconscious" minds, stored in our brain's file cabinet, and we become so accustomed to being controlled by our patterns that we cannot notice them unless someone teaches us how to do so.*

4. *If you are not fulfilling your potential, it is probably because an unproductive pattern in your unconscious mind is getting in the way, sapping your energy, or even taking over entire areas of your life.*

5. *When you make your patterns "conscious" and learn to notice them, you can break the unproductive ones by applying a very clear step-by-step, do-it-yourself method.*

6. *When you break your unproductive patterns and become aware of the moments when fate puts a chute or a ladder right in your path, you can make the leap to pursuing better opportunities in love, work, school, and anything else.*

That's my understanding of the psychoanalytic theory and method in a nutshell (so to speak). It's very simple, really. The following chapters of this book take what I learned in my twenty-five years in this field, and offer it to you in the form of a step-by-step, self-guided technique, along with important knowledge explained in a clear way that can be applied to your own life.

Maybe the lessons you learn from this book will take some effort to apply and might even feel unnatural at first. But practice them enough and you will be on your way to fulfilling your untapped potential for success and happiness.

If you sense that you have unfulfilled potential, reading this book will help you to look at your life with a fresh and objective eye. It will help you notice the traps of detouring patterns so that you can avoid them. And it will help you notice the opportunities when they knock so that you can take advantage of them. Never before has this important information been available in a form that is so easy to understand and apply.

CHAPTER 2

What are Patterns?

A PATTERN IS a series of active steps that we follow the same way, in the same order, all the time. If we follow a certain pattern enough times, it becomes automatic. It gets to a point where we can carry out the series of steps without even thinking about them. Eventually, the pattern becomes second nature to us. It becomes a part of our usual routines.

Like it or not, patterns just happen. They are habitual. This is because human beings have an instinct to do what is familiar without giving it much thought. We instinctively return to the familiar. Being creatures of habit, we find comfort in taking the same route from home to work, eating the same kinds of food we usually eat, shopping at the same market, revisiting our favorite restaurants, and spending time at our same vacation spot. If we do something enough it can become a pattern. And patterns are hard to break. They've become programmed into us.

I guarantee that you are following patterns every day, probably without even knowing it. Patterns can be found in how we communicate, how we work, and how we relate to those we desire and those we love. We have patterns of how we act when we are sick and cope when we are upset, of how we meet challenges and deal with disappointment. We have patterns of eating, sleeping, and taking care (or not taking care) of ourselves. And we have patterns of how we deal with money matters, how we act in a family, how we approach school, and how we proceed with our careers. Patterns can be helpful, or they can cause problems. We may have helpful patterns in some areas of life and problematic patterns in others.

Patterns can be small and insignificant, or large and important. Our morning routines often consist of insignificant patterns we carry out without much thought. The way we wash, brush our teeth, comb our hair, dress, eat breakfast, feed the dog, take the kids to school, grab a cup of coffee, read the paper, listen to the news, get into our cars, or take a bus or train, and commute to work or school, are all patterns. We generally do these activities in a similar way every day, or at least every weekday. Patterns can help us get through the humdrum parts of life more easily and efficiently. And usually, by relying on our patterns, most of us get where we are going pretty much on time, or only a few minutes late.

Without patterns, we would be required to think about every little step and decision, and we would be constantly preoccupied with small details. Patterns act as shortcuts. It's like putting a plane on automatic pilot, or a car on cruise control. As long as conditions are unchallenging, and these unchallenging conditions stay pretty much the same, no further adjustment is needed for a while.

Good Patterns, Bad Patterns

I want to make it clear that not all patterns are bad for us. As a matter of fact, sometimes patterns are life saving. I owe my life to a helpful pattern that I learned when I was in my twenties. Back then, I went to a martial arts class several times a week. I learned that when you are met with an immovable force, you can still win if you relax and go with the flow. "A branch that bends cannot break" is what we were taught. We practiced this pattern in every class during our sparring exercises. Eventually, relaxing and bending became a pattern for me when faced with an onslaught that couldn't be overcome by opposition.

One day I was driving on a highway in France when a truck driver in the next lane fell asleep, lost control of his truck, and literally ran over my car. The impact was sudden.

Instinctively I relaxed and bent like a branch going with the flow of the impact. The driver's-side door and roof areas were crushed, leaving the windows pulverized, but I leaned over into the passenger side at the moment of impact and survived—thanks to a helpful pattern.

Most patterns are harmless, many are helpful time-savers, and, as I just pointed out, some are lifesavers. But other patterns can become huge obstacles to accomplishing your goals. Patterns that don't work in your favor can prevent you from achieving important goals in your love life, family life, school life, creative life, or work life. When these problem patterns take over, the result is a series of missed opportunities and setbacks.

Even seemingly insignificant patterns can lead people in the wrong direction. For instance, one of my patients had a problem with her morning routine. It involved too many steps, and took so long that she was often late for work. No matter what time she woke up, and no matter how late she was for work, she still had to go through a long and complicated ritual. Once the pattern was in action she couldn't stop it. She had to use all the lotions and potions and creams and rinses on her agenda or she didn't feel quite right. She felt she had no control over this routine that made her take longer and forever caused her to be late.

This is a simple example of a pattern that detours someone from a goal rather than acting as a shortcut. Her pattern was easy to determine, but not all of our unhelpful patterns are as obvious and easy to identify as that of my lotion-and-potion patient. And the consequences of repeating them could be much more serious than being habitually late.

If Jane really wants to find a man who is good "husband material," but she keeps ending up with guys who are afraid of commitment, there's a good chance she's following a problematic pattern in her love life without even knowing it. If Ted is trying to be a good father but keeps finding himself frustrated and yelling at his kids, there's a good chance he's following a problematic pattern in his family life without knowing it. If Mary is trying to become a partner in her law firm but never seems to get the credit she deserves when she "saves the day," there's a good chance she's following a pattern in her career without knowing it.

When Your Best Effort Isn't Good Enough

When the goal you seek always seems to be out of reach despite your best efforts, it is time to think about whether there might be an unhelpful pattern in your life that is taking over and controlling the outcomes without your even realizing it.

When a pattern is in control, you miss the chance to avoid problems, and you also miss the chance to take advantage of opportunities. When you miss both important chances, you are at a *big* disadvantage.

When a pilot puts a plane on automatic pilot but suddenly there is a lot of turbulence, it is not prudent to let the autopilot control the flight. It is better if the pilot is aware of each changing condition and makes executive decisions to respond and adjust in the right way to get to the destination safely and efficiently.

If a pattern overrides your ability to notice and respond to changing conditions—to those inevitable appearances of chutes and ladders—you become unable to adjust in the right ways. It is like turning on "cruise control" in your car and then forgetting about paying attention to the road or noticing a "construction ahead" or "detour" sign. Long delays, and maybe even a crash, won't be far off. Crashes in love, at work, and at home are usually caused by a similar reliance on a pattern of "cruise control."

When we are participating in our patterns, we may not always notice the conditions around us, what other people are doing, saying, thinking or feeling. And worse yet, when we are deeply involved participating in unproductive patterns we may not always notice what we are thinking, feeling, or picking up about others until it is too late and something has gone wrong.

How can you tell if you are approaching important situations in a patterned way? How can you figure out if you automatically follow a habitual series of steps in some area of your life? And how can you figure out if the pattern you are following is helpful to you or harmful?

The answer is actually very simple:

If the outcome tends not to be the one you want, or if you seem to be delayed for no reason, or if your efforts typically suffer a setback along the way, then there is a good chance you are following an unhelpful pattern without even knowing it.

To illustrate, let's look at a more important pattern in life than the morning routine. Each of us has our own pattern for how to deal with disappointment or defeat. Some people follow the adage, "Get right back on the horse that threw you." These folks pick themselves up from defeat and get back on track immediately. Other people—actually most of us—have to do something to soothe themselves before moving ahead.

Take the example of being criticized for a failed project at work. Jim may respond to this by going to the batting cage and hitting pitches for an hour. Joan may go home and binge on a gallon of Häagen-Dazs ice cream. Bev might go home and get into a terrible fight with her husband over nothing in particular. And Max might drown his sorrows in a fifth of vodka that was chilling in the freezer, and miss the next day of work

Each of us has a characteristic way of dealing with impor-tant issues and events in life. When we have a characteristic way of doing something, that's a pattern. If the pattern is a good one, things work out well. But if the pattern is problematic we are thrown off course, we do unproductive things, and we end up delaying progress toward our goals. Worse yet, we might crash, and slip even farther away from our goals!

Furthermore, there are some situations we all face in which patterns, even helpful ones, are no good at all. This is because there are some things in life that cannot be accomplished if you approach them the same way every time. There are certain accomplishments that you may only attain by adjusting as you go along, noticing the changing conditions as they occur, and taking advantage of them. There are certain goals that can only be achieved if you are able to break all your old patterns associated with that area of your life.

For instance, in forming love relationships, remaining flexible allows you to notice and adjust to that special new person in your life. And, in pursuing new career endeavors, remaining adaptable allows you to adjust to new co-workers, tasks, and bosses. When conditions are changing, you have to be free of patterns in order to do what is needed to move ahead to the next level. Sometimes what worked to get from point A to point B is not going to work to get from point B to point C. This is also true in raising children, since they are changing all the time as they grow up and require parents to adjust their approaches constantly.

Patterns can get in the way of adjusting. Eventually, if we fall short of accomplishing our goals often enough, these patterns start to define our lives and give us a reputation of underachievement in one or more important areas. This can take a heavy toll since we all know we are prone to "live up" (or down, as the case may be) to our reputations.

Despite our best efforts, it sometimes seems we can't stop ourselves from heading down the garden path another time. Or we don't even notice the pattern until it is too late to avoid it. Doing something as natural as following our gut instincts can land us in the same eerily familiar, and undesirable, circumstance.

De-Mystify Your Life

How come these patterns are so mysterious and hard to pin down? Why don't we notice them and correct ourselves and have more success? Why do we repeat a pattern that has proven unproductive?

Psychoanalysts have been studying these questions for a hundred years and have discovered some answers. The short answer to why patterns are so mysterious is that they live in a hidden part of us. They live in the unconscious mind.

Can we be taught to see our patterns? Can we find reasons why we repeat them? And, can we take back control? The answer to all of these questions is, "Yes, most definitely, yes."

CHAPTER 3

The Secret Life of Patterns

⁓

PATTERNS LIVE A secret life inside of you. They are hiding in your mind. Like undercover agents, these patterns have gone undiscovered and have affected your decisions without you or anyone else noticing—possibly for a long time.

To quote the classic Chinese proverb, "If you know your enemy and know yourself, you can fight a hundred battles without disaster." Likewise, if you understand your pattern, you'll be able to identify the weak links in its chain and be better able to break it.

To understand your patterns, you have to begin by thinking about things you probably haven't thought much about in a long time. As adults we often forget about the magic of secrets and the wonder of mysterious things. Secrets and mysteries were very real and exciting when we were children. Sometimes they were enjoyable and sometimes downright fearsome. Playing hide-and-seek, for instance, is just one example of how hiding and discovery were more a part of our childhood experiences than our adult lives. The childhood excitement of discovering and taking advantage of a shortcut is another example. Somehow, as we grow up, this magic drops out of our everyday vocabulary and disappears from our everyday thoughts.

There is nothing particularly magical about patterns except for their "now you see it, now you don't" aspect. *The real magic is to make these invisible phantoms visible.* And, to accomplish this, you will need to reactivate your childhood interest in uncovering secrets. This chapter will reveal three very important things about the secret life of patterns (three things that your patterns *don't* want you to know because these things will threaten their control over you):

1. *Where your patterns reside.*
2. *What motivates patterns to continue to carry out their mission (of holding us back).*
3. *The wasted energy that goes into following our patterns.*

Secret #1:
Where Patterns Reside

The unconscious part of our minds is the part that exists

below the level of our usual and *conscious* awareness. The only way that problematic patterns can keep controlling us is if they live undiscovered, hidden in our unconscious minds where we can't see them. If we can't see them, then we can't understand them. Nor can we evaluate whether they are helping or hurting our success. If we can't see them or evaluate them, then certainly we are powerless to change them. If our patterns were not hidden from our view and were visible to us in our conscious minds, we'd certainly weed out the ones that didn't make sense.

Let's look at the difference between the conscious mind, with which most of us are pretty familiar, and the unconscious mind, which is more of a mystery.

The conscious mind is where we keep old and new information we aren't hiding from ourselves. The conscious mind could include our shopping lists, daily worries, gossip, and recent conversations. It could include movies we've seen or books we've read, work assignments, and directions to work or school. It could include recollections of last year's summer vacation, or of friends we had in college, or of some childhood memories. The conscious mind is a file cabinet of all the things we can think of or remember if we try.

On the other hand, the unconscious mind is like having an invisible folder in the operating system of your computer—the contents of which affect the operation of the machine but you just can't see into it. Because we are unaware of it, we generally operate as if this portion simply does not exist.

This means we are completely oblivious of some of the contents of our own minds even if those contents affect us in significant ways. It is sometimes a hard concept to swallow, especially at first.

This important fact is very well known to psychoanalysts and not so well known to everybody else. Psychoanalysts think of the mind along the same lines as we think of an iceberg. Some of it is above the surface and easy to notice, and a good portion of it is below the surface and takes some effort to explore. Remember that the *Titanic* was done in by an iceberg hidden below the surface. In the same way, our patterns have the same hidden ability to sabotage and stop us from reaching our life goals.

How does someone find something that has remained invisible? The answer is to have the right tools, a spirit of exploration, and then to look on a different level or in a different way. To investigate the undersea portion of an iceberg requires cold-water diving gear, education in the use of those tools, and a spirit of exploration. Similarly, to investigate seemingly invisible causes of certain health problems, such as viruses and bacteria, you need to use such tools as a high-powered microscope, and to be educated in the use of that equipment. You need an open mind, and you especially need a spirit of exploration.

A very courageous spirit of exploration was required for the first explorers who ventured into unknown places. Think of those brave souls who first made it to the North Pole or the South Pole, who climbed Mount Everest or walked on the moon. They explored the most unknown places in our outside world. To find your patterns also requires a courageous spirit of exploration, as you will be exploring your inner world and you don't know beforehand exactly what patterns you are going to find.

Secret #2:
The Motive of All Patterns

When a pattern seems to have no rhyme or reason, when it leads to a lifestyle that doesn't fulfill our goals and when it prevents us from realizing our potential, our continued participation in it defies all logic. As we learned, part of the explanation is that patterns reside in the unconscious, so that we don't notice them. But another part of the explanation is that patterns are driven by a very powerful motivator. That motivator has to be so strong that it overrides our common sense, leads us to disregard the consequences, and drives us to continue the pattern that has already proven to be unproductive.

The motivator for continuing a problematic pattern is the deeply held conviction, even if we are not aware of having it, that following the pattern will get us something we dearly want. We believe that following the pattern will help us to complete an important piece of unfinished business or will help us to accomplish a long awaited goal.

By having the conviction that the pattern will accomplish something good for us, even if this conviction resides in the unconscious mind, we are giving that pattern carte blanche to proceed undaunted.

Don't be fooled when people try to convince you that your love life or your work life is going in circles because you *want* to suffer or because you are lazy. Don't accept that you are a masochist or have low self-esteem or no discipline. If people try to tell you that you are stuck in a rut because you have a fear of success, don't believe them.

Contrary to the standard folk wisdom, problematic patterns are *not* driven by some weakness in your character! Problematic patterns are all driven by the conviction that following the pattern is the way to achieve something.

Isn't it ironic that patterns of underachievement are motivated by a desire to achieve? But that is, in fact, the situation. All unproductive patterns are motivated by a good intention.

We all want to have the best lives we can. You don't wake up in the morning and say to yourself, "Today, I am going to participate in unproductive patterns so that I can impede my progress toward my goals." We do the things we do because we have good intentions. Things go wrong when those good intentions are enacted through the vehicle of misguided patterns.

However, there is one positive aspect to continually repeating patterns that keep you from fulfilling your potential. Your effort shows you've got optimism. It shows that you've got the hopeful belief that things will work out if you keep trying. That optimism is very important. It is at the core of every human endeavor. And it is an optimism that, harnessed properly, can become the key ingredient to success.

In the case of patterns, the motivating optimism usually resides where the patterns reside, in the unconscious mind. Therefore, you may not be in touch with the feeling of optimism that drives you to repeat problematic patterns. But the optimistic hope is there. Reading this book, for instance, is a testimony to the fact that you have this optimism and gumption inside of you. You are probably reading in order to help yourself or to help someone else. This type of optimism has its roots in our developing years, when mastering little challenges was what life was all about.

To illustrate, let's look at a little scene that occurred in my house when my daughter was just two years old. I watched as she took her crayon and put it in the cup holder in the arm of her plastic chair. The cup holder had a round hole at the bottom and the crayon fell through the hole. She watched as the crayon disappeared, listened to it rattle as it fell through the innards of the hollow plastic chair, then found it again as it emerged from the hollow bottom frame of the chair and reappeared on the floor.

When she found the crayon, she picked it up, and without missing a beat put the crayon back in the cup holder in the arm of the chair, listened to it rattle through the innards, and picked it up off the floor—and then she began the process all over again. This continued, over and over, for quite some time.

As a psychoanalyst, I couldn't help but think about Freud's last important writing of his career, in which he talked about observing a young child roll a spool of thread under a dresser, watch it disappear, and then look for it and retrieve it, over and over again. Watching this child and the spool of thread made Freud's mind click.

Up until this point, Freud believed that there were two basic things that drove people's behavior. These were the life instinct (creative, loving, or self-preservative) and the death instinct (inert, hateful, or self-destructive). But, shortly before his death, Freud decided that these two basic drives seemed pale in comparison to the powerful drive to repeat, which he called the "repetition compulsion." Freud decided that this urge to repeat was "stronger than the will to live, and stronger than the fear of death." So the urge to repeat patterns is not going to be an easy urge to break.

My daughter, and Freud's boy with the spool, both had the outcome they were after. My daughter dropped the crayon into the abyss in order to feel the joy of achievement upon finding it. And she continued dropping the crayon and finding it again in order to feel the further joy of another achievement. "It was darkest and then came the dawn"—or then came the crayon, in this instance. No matter how many times the crayon was "lost," a basic optimism told her the goal of seeing that crayon again was indeed possible.

However, this is the ideal scenario, where what is lost is once again found and the situation works out as one planned—where trying repeatedly leads to a *mastery experience.* In search of a similar experience of mastery as adults, many of us might repeat a pattern, even if it means repeating the same mistake in life over and over again, because there is hope that it will work out right someday.

Patterns are motivated by the optimistic hope that a mastery experience will result sooner or later, even if it is much, much later. Because of the strength of the *compulsion to repeat,* which is a part of human nature, sometimes we don't even pay attention to the fact that trying the same thing, in the same way, over and over again, simply will not get us the outcome we desire.

There is optimism in trying to get a better outcome and in the hope that if you repeat the loop enough times, the action will get you out of the loop. Of course, this is usually fallacious thinking since, when we are participating in patterns, optimistic repeating can go on for years without success. Staying in the same loop keeps you in the same loop, no matter how optimistic you are about anything different happening.

What is it that we seek when we repeat a life pattern or the same mistake over and over? What on earth are we looking for when the same kind of career problem, or the same kind of relationship problem, or the same kind of money problem, does us in, again and again?

What we are seeking is usually something pretty basic when one comes right down to it. We are seeking love, success, pride, appreciation, companionship, achievement, self-esteem, happiness, and so on. We might be seeking one of these things because we lost it somewhere in the past, and it has been something we always had hoped to regain. Or we might be seeking one of these things because it was something we have always wanted but never had.

Patterns are not generally motivated by something petty, or something of which to be ashamed. Patterns are usually motivated by the desire to retrieve or obtain something worthwhile, something any reasonable person would consider very important.

The point here is that problematic patterns are motivated by an attempt to achieve a mastery outcome over something very important to us. They are *always* based on optimism, even if our optimism is wrongly placed. Optimism is the basis of all striving to improve our lives.

Finding out that you have been hoping and repeating within a pattern that cannot succeed is the bad news. But the fact that you are trying means you have hope of improving your life. And the fact that you are repeating means you have energy. The good news is that you have the raw material of optimism needed for success. It means the energy to succeed is in you; it just has to be properly directed out of the loop.

Secret #3:
Patterns Eat Up Our Productive Energy

We are all born with a certain amount of life energy installed in us. Thankfully, it's usually enough to last a lifetime. Barring any premature tragedies, we come packed with sufficient energy to have a lively, vibrant life from beginning to end. If our lives are not lively, vibrant, and energetic, it might mean that our energy is not being used correctly or that something is draining our energy.

To appreciate how you can make your life as vibrant as possible, it is important to understand some basics about the energy that powers you. This is the third, and final, prerequisite to understanding the secret life of patterns.

Psychoanalysts believe that our energy is "factory installed" and present at birth. Furthermore, they believe that, like a rechargeable battery, there is the possibility of reinvigorating our energy from time to time and draining it from time to time. Sleep or vacation or happiness or success can recharge it, and stress or participating in unproductive patterns can drain our energy.

If you happen to leave your car's headlights on overnight, you'll wake to find that the battery is low or that the car won't even start because energy was used up without your realizing it. Participating in unproductive patterns similarly uses up energy without our knowledge and can leave us feeling less energetic than we should be feeling.

Life is short, and it is important that we have our full energy at our disposal to accomplish the goals we want, and to enjoy having achieved these goals during our lifetime. This means it is very important for us to decide about exactly how we use the energy we have.

Psychoanalysts think about the behavior of our energies in much the same way that we all think about the behavior of water. Like water, it can be contained somewhere. And, furthermore, it can be poured from one container to another, back and forth. If we are given one full glass of water, we can, for instance, pour half of it into one glass and half into another. Or we can pour two-thirds in one glass and one-third in another, and so on. Psychoanalysts think about our goals as the containers for this water. We can choose how to distribute it or how much energy to pour into each goal.

When it comes to our life energy, the most important thing is how we distribute it. The way we distribute determines the chances we have for a successful life. It is even part of our everyday language to talk about the things we want to "put our energy into." There are two basic ways that we distribute our life energies: *productively* and *unproductively*.

Dream the *Possible* Dream

Some people achieve their life goals and some people don't. People who are successful and fulfilled tend to pour the majority of their energy into activities that accomplish their life goals. People who are undersuccessful and underfulfilled tend to pour the majority of their energy into patterns which, if carried out, will not accomplish anything productive. Distributing precious energy into unproductive patterns is a waste.

When we think of Don Quixote charging at windmills, it all seems rather humorous. But think about it . . . What if Don Quixote dreamed a *possible* dream and put the majority of his energy into pursuing it? Imagine what he could have accomplished. Now, imagine what you can accomplish if you take back the energy that goes into your patterns (your personal quixotic windmills) and put your full energy into your *intentional* goals!

CHAPTER 4

The Uphill Struggle to Fulfill Potential

⌣

TO ILLUSTRATE HOW patterns can secretly exercise control over someone's life and interfere with achievement, let's briefly examine the case of Joe.

Joe is a forty-something businessman who sees himself as having the potential to be a high-powered leader in his manufacturing industry.[1] Indeed, when Joe came to talk with me and explained his ideas, it was clear that he possessed a brilliant vision. He had a plan that would accomplish the dual business goals of production facility safety and corporate

---

[1] This and all other case histories in this book are based on real cases but all are composites of several people's cases that best illustrate the points I want to communicate. In telling these stories, all identities, names, places, professions, and other identifying information have been changed to protect my patients' confidentiality and honor the trust that they have placed in me.

growth. For his industry, in which safety seemed pitted against corporate profits, his vision could be transformative and a win-win scenario.

Despite his strong potential, Joe remained at the "worker bee" level and couldn't rise to a leadership position. He was always a "second banana," as he put it, never offered the chance to manage a department or project. When his boss finally took up the banner of Joe's "safe and profitable" program, it put the company at the head of the pack in terms of both public safety and profits by incorporating a new manufacturing process.

Normally, that accomplishment would lead to increased corporate recognition or expanded responsibilities for the mastermind of such a program, but neither happened for Joe. For him, obtaining the recognition he truly deserved was an uphill struggle.

We already know that when a person's potential and accomplishments don't match, there are probably unproductive patterns at play. Joe sensed he had the qualities to be a good leader. This feeling resided in his conscious awareness—which is equivalent to the visible portion of the iceberg. But as we have learned, the tip of the iceberg is not where patterns reside.

Joe was baffled that someone with his unique vision and ability to problem-solve was not more successful. He was bothered because he couldn't put his finger on what was going wrong. Since people usually believe that the tip of the iceberg, the part of their own minds that they can readily see, is the whole thing, the visible evidence just didn't add up.

Joe now had tangible evidence of his abilities in his own accomplishments at his company. Since this and his personal belief in his potential represented the totality of his self-awareness in the work world, the additional fact that his efforts hadn't achieved recognition was completely incomprehensible. Being overlooked for this breakthrough vision felt downright unfair.

What You Don't Know Can Hurt You

What Joe didn't know about himself could, and did, hurt him. There were certain things going on in Joe's unconscious mind that worked against fulfilling his potential. There are more facts to consider than those that were available to Joe's conscious awareness. According to Secret #1, Joe's pattern would reside in his unconscious mind, and would control him without his awareness.

Although he didn't realize it, many of Joe's activities were aimed at seeking the recognition of his colleagues and others in his industry. This behavior stemmed from his long-standing and unproductive pattern of trying to get a "pat on the head," and looking toward others—especially those in authority above him—for this sort of reinforcement.

Having a desire for recognition is not necessarily a problem. However, if that desire is expressed in an automatic behavior pattern, and evidence of that desire leaks out in one's behavior in uncontrolled ways that telegraph one's insecurities, there can be problems.

As we learned in Secret #2, the motive of all patterns is to gain something or achieve mastery over something important in our lives. Joe's pattern, though faulty in its execution, was motivated by a drive to seek the recognition he deserved. Joe was clearly an unsung hero. He hoped to gain reassurance that he was doing a good job. And isn't that something he deserved? Certainly it was.

Patterns Waste Your Talent

By definition, a pattern is a series of active steps that we follow the same way, in the same order, all the time. Followed often enough, these patterns become automatic. What we discover when examining Joe's work life is a consistent series of active steps that he unwittingly followed. His pattern always started in the same way: there was a challenge to be met, Joe rose to the challenge, he produced a brilliant solution, and he passed on that solution to his colleagues or superiors.

However, before anyone had a chance to test out his solution, and before anyone could reflect on what a great contribution Joe had made, Joe's motive to obtain recognition drove him to another action step in his pattern—a very unproductive one. That action step was to remind everyone that he was responsible for the solution and to hint repeatedly that he was looking for feedback about his good work.

Whenever Joe interacted with his boss or others in his company, he always boasted about his latest good idea in a way that was reminiscent of an insecure school kid fishing for compliments. It was as if he were always tugging on someone's coat sleeve and saying, "Look what a good job I did! Hey, didn't I do a great job? Didn't I? Didn't I?" By acting in a manner unbecoming for a leader, he automatically predisposed his colleagues to think less of him. This made it completely unlikely that those in power over him would take the time to reflect on Joe's accomplishment or reward him for it.

It didn't matter that Joe had made a great contribution with his "safe and profitable" manufacturing program. And it didn't earn him points that the program was instituted in all of his company's manufacturing facilities. What mattered most was the way in which he kept bringing it up in front of everyone.

Joe carried out the pattern of flaunting his accomplishments because he was motivated by the unconsciously held idea that if he repeated the pattern enough times, he'd eventually get that recognition. The steps of the pattern were so deeply ingrained in his unconscious mind that they could be

carried out on automatic pilot. The optimism that participating in his unproductive pattern would lead to eventual
mastery was quite strong. Joe's pattern persuaded him that,
maybe the very next time, doing the same thing in the same
wrong-minded way would finally accomplish his goal.

To add insult to injury, the last action step in Joe's pattern
all but sealed his fate in his work environment. When Joe
didn't get that sought-after attention, he pouted. He only
pouted a little bit, but still he visibly pouted. He pouted so
little that it happened below Joe's own radar. Yet to others,
he seemed just the slightest bit peeved, somewhat less polite,
maybe even a little curt. He withdrew slightly from his colleagues and worked with his office door closed while he
licked his wounds. But since patterns are unconscious, Joe
didn't know he was doing anything that was perceptible to
others. He wasn't even aware of feeling troubled.

A lot of what happens between people in human interac-
tion occurs on an intuitive level. Joe's colleagues and superiors may not have read Joe's behaviors clearly, but they may
have intuited something about him—and reacted to it on
the basis of instinct alone—without giving it any further
thought. Whether those around Joe were reacting with conscious awareness or reacting instinctively didn't matter, since
the devastating effect on his career was the same. From the
point of view of his bosses, colleagues, and other people in
his industry, Joe was a good worker, but he just wasn't
someone they took seriously or trusted as a leader.

According to Secret #3 about patterns, an additional consequence of participating in unproductive patterns is that it diverts precious energy away from productive pursuits. Recognition-seeking is one type of unproductive pattern into which our energies might be poured and thereby wasted.

In Joe's case, whenever he failed in his efforts to receive recognition, he took a long period of time to recover from the rejection. He became passive, preoccupied, and unable to work productively for days at a time. Joe's constant repetition of his unproductive pattern (his version of charging at windmills) left him drained at the end of each pattern cycle. Such a pattern would leave anyone drained. Look at all the effort that went into the steps of brainstorming, ineffectively self-promoting, and coping with disappointment and frustration.

Don't Do It!

Now we can see how a person with tremendous potential becomes unable to succeed. Joe's story is proof that *if we cannot put our best foot forward in our day-to-day lives, it is because we are unwittingly living out our unproductive patterns.*

All of us want to be recognized when we do a good job. It's part of being human. As is usually the case in good people, Joe's motive was a good one. He was repeatedly robbed of this recognition, and he wanted to gain mastery by making sure he didn't get robbed again.

By the time Joe came to talk to me, he was doubting himself and questioning his abilities and goals. This happens to many talented people who are caught in the grip of unproductive patterns. Eventually, even the strongest of us gets worn down by patterns and their bad effects. Then self-doubt creeps in. I explained to Joe, just as I'm explaining it to you now, that it doesn't have to be this way.

Unproductive patterns can wear you down and make you doubt your potential or even lead you to adjust your goals downward.

Don't do it!

Don't settle for less of a life! Instead, there is a method you can apply to break those unproductive patterns so that you can fulfill your potential. I shared that method with Joe. And, now I'm going to share that method with you.

CHAPTER 5

Pattern Breaking for Everyone: The SUBGAP Method

THERE ARE ONLY four important steps to fulfilling your potential by breaking the patterns that hold you back. Each of these steps brings you closer to achieving your potential. The four steps which are required to break your patterns and keep them broken for the rest of your life are:

> **S**eeing,
> **U**nderstanding,
> **B**reaking, and
> **G**uarding
> **A**gainst
> **P**atterns

The acronym for the four leaps is S-U-B-G-A-P, and therefore I call this the SUBGAP method. It is the clear and basic step-by-step approach that I have developed and practiced in treating my patients. It is the method that I've taught to my students; it is the method that I used to break my own patterns. By applying this approach, you will be walking in the footsteps of the many people who have already used it successfully. This will make your journey faster, more effective, and far more likely to bring you success and fulfillment.

You don't have to reinvent the wheel! I am going to teach you everything you need to know in the upcoming chapters. *It is probably the most worthwhile information you could ever absorb.*

The SUBGAP method provides you with the knowledge and techniques to: *see* your unproductive pattern when you might never have been able to see it before; *understand* exactly how this pattern operates in the greater whole of your life (what opportunities it hides and what setbacks it lures you into); *break* your unproductive pattern by taking a decisive action that counteracts it and sets you on a direct path toward your goals; and, *guard against patterns* for the rest of your life by developing a "Pattern-Proof Mindset."

Ready to Begin?

Are you ready to learn how to fulfill your potential? It's quite a journey you are about to embark upon. It may be a journey you sensed you needed to make, but just didn't know how to begin. It may be a journey you have all but given up on making. So, don't be surprised if you have questions about whether fulfilling your potential is even possible. It is only natural if you are skeptical about how well you can understand or use this method.

As we begin, let me reassure you that:

- If you are not fulfilling your potential in an area of your life, you are not the problem, your pattern is holding you back.
- No pattern is beyond detection, no matter how long it has been hidden.
- The SUBGAP process will not be hard to understand or apply.
- Fulfilling your potential is not out of reach.

The beauty of the SUBGAP method is that it progresses step-by-step. You don't have to worry about taking on too much at once or getting in above your head. And you don't have to brace yourself for any sudden shocks. As a matter of fact, big changes in your patterns and leaps in your fulfillment have the best chances of being permanent improvements if they occur gradually. Just take each of the four steps of the SUBGAP method one at a time, and you will be following the best possible path to achieving your potential.

PART TWO

Seeing

⸙

Vision is the art of seeing things invisible.
—Jonathan Swift

CHAPTER 6

Learning to See
Your Patterns

THE FIRST STEP in the SUBGAP method is *seeing*. Learning to see your unproductive patterns is very much like solving the visual puzzle, "What's wrong with this picture?" Think of one of those pictures where a discrepant element is somewhere in the landscape. At first, that element does not stand out. It is there in the picture but, since we can't see it right away, it is invisible to us—at least temporarily. After we study the picture for a while, however, the one thing that is out of place becomes perfectly clear.

The first prerequisite to breaking your unproductive patterns is learning to see your patterns. Only after that will you be able to take on the task of changing those patterns.

Patterns that are holding you back in your daily life can seem invisible—until you apply a proven method to find them. First of all, you need to identify the area of your life that is not as "on track" as you sense it could be, or "less than" it should be. And once you know the general area of underful-fillment in your life, you'll have to look more closely to discover exactly what pattern is going on there and how it is causing you to miss out.

What's Missing in Your Life?

Is there a hard-to-explain inconsistency in your life? For instance, are you able to use your people skills at your job, but your personal relationships don't work out well? Do you find yourself setting good goals but accomplishing less than you think you should? Are you always working hard but never getting ahead financially or not getting enough recognition at work? Do opportunities pass you by and you kick yourself afterward for not saying or doing the right thing and "striking while the iron was hot"?

Are you great at advising others but can't make the same advice work for yourself? Are you a person with much to give but no one to give to? Or someone who gives all the time but doesn't get much back? Do you try your best to change things for the better but feel your voice isn't heard? Or are you a bit disappointed in yourself and how you live your life, instead of proud of yourself for behaving the way you admire?

If you are like most people, you may have gotten used to living with something important being missing from your life. Many of us become so accustomed to underfulfillment that we literally take it for granted and don't *see* what is robbing us of success, achievement, happiness, satisfaction in work, contentment in love, and comfort with ourselves.

What is the best way to see the problematic element in your life? You need to take a scientific approach similar to the scientific eye that psychoanalysts apply to uncover people's patterns.

Hunting for your own patterns will require you to learn how to conduct good, useful research on yourself. We are not accustomed to seeing ourselves objectively. But the objective view is necessary if we're going to see what's missing or out of place, and to recognize our unproductive patterns.

Scientific vs. Fatalistic?

When I say that you need to take a scientific approach, I do not mean that you must put yourself in a laboratory or run a series of tests. You do not have to get cold and clinical. And you won't have to learn any complicated theories or formulas.

A scientific approach makes good use of expert knowledge and takes a comprehensive look at all the facts, including hard-to-find ones, in order to draw the best and most objective conclusions. But most of us do not take a very scientific approach to thinking about our lives. More often, we take a philosophical approach—thinking in terms of "this was (or was not) meant to be." We become fatalistic. Many people may accept or curse their fate, but they don't believe they can change it. Still others may embrace an all-consuming approach, believing that everything will turn out all right if they just focus intensely on a single decision, project, or relationship to the exclusion of all else. And, of course, there are those of us who approach life without giving it much thought at all.

People tend to think of their lives and goals as being so complex and mysterious that it would be impossible to narrow problems down to a solvable simple series of action steps.

How do we accomplish the monumental feat of figuring out, among the millions of facts about our lives, where our patterns are hidden?

A Simple Scientific Method

The best way to find out what is really happening in your life is to research that situation from two perspectives at once. These two perspectives are known as the *top-down* approach and the *bottom-up* approach. Indeed, the *seeing* step in the SUBGAP method requires a combination of these two approaches.

By applying these two perspectives, you will be maximizing

the chance of discovering your pattern, and that missing link responsible for your underfulfillment will be unable to escape detection.

What do I mean by "top down" and "bottom up"? To explain, let me give you an example from another field of investigation.

When researchers at the Center for Disease Control (CDC) investigate outbreaks of illness, they use this double-sided scientific method to ensure that they get to the root of the problem and solve it as quickly as possible.

First of all, there's the top-down investigation—bringing to bear the existing scientific knowledge to shed light on outbreaks of illness. An important piece of scientific knowledge that CDC researchers apply is the "germ theory of transmission." The germ theory is a well-known and basic assumption in modern medicine that tells us that the vehicle by which disease spreads is likely to be a virus, bacteria, toxin, or genetic defect.

If there is an outbreak of serious illness in Smalltown, USA, our existing knowledge tells us that the affected people probably contracted a virus, bacteria, or toxin in the vicinity of Smalltown, USA. This top-down information tells us where to look and a little bit about exactly what to look for. But why did the outbreak start here? Why did it hit Smalltown, and not a neighboring town? A different type of scientific approach is needed to find these more specific answers.

Once the top-down information has been applied and the CDC researchers have narrowed down the area of the country to be studied and narrowed down what kind of thing they are seeking, then the researchers apply a bottom-up approach. This means that they go about the business of fact-finding, gathering and examining the details of a specific situation to discover what conclusions can be drawn. So CDC researchers catch the next plane to the pinpointed town and start asking questions.

The CDC researchers canvas the local hospitals and find all the affected people. They interview them and find out what common workplaces, activities, or eating spots everyone shared. Bottom-up research is a fact-finding mission; it is investigative reporting; it is top-notch detective work worthy of Sherlock Holmes.

When CDC researchers cull through hundreds of facts they can ultimately discover a relationship between all the victims. If they note that all the people hospitalized for this illness recently had a meal at the local Pappy Burger, then the data means that something is probably amiss regarding the food, food-handling, or staff at Pappy Burger, which needs to be examined and corrected. Applying a bottom-up approach helps researchers to discover a pattern among all the facts in the region that have been top-down pinpointed for investigation.

Once the pattern between the facts begins to show, further research can be performed on the food, employees, and kitchen at that restaurant, tests conducted, and the problem discovered and resolved so that the cycle of illness does not repeat.

Without applying this top-down/bottom-up method for identifying the cause of illness, all we would know is that some people in Smalltown, USA, became ill. We wouldn't know why, we wouldn't see the relationship between the facts (the pattern) and we couldn't correct it. Therefore, the problem could and would easily happen again.

Your Scientific Eye

When you take a scientific approach to looking at the area of underfulfillment or underachievement in your life, you will be saying:

- This fate for me is *not* written in the stars.
- Even if it is a mystery to me now, I can find an answer scientifically.
- If I'm not living up to my potential in a certain area of my life, it's the result of patterns that are holding me back.
- I know that I can use the SUBGAP method to detect, understand, and break my unproductive patterns.
- I can choose to take steps to break those patterns.
- Once I've done that, I no longer need to be in the grip of forces beyond my control, and the result will be a much more satisfying life.

By saying this to yourself you are taking the first step in the *seeing* process—you have made a very big leap. You have now gone from taking your life for granted (where the facts of your life swirl around your head) to looking at your life in a more scientific manner which can give you control over your future.

Your Top-Down Pattern Hunt

When it comes to something as elusive as patterns, you might not even believe that you have them or that they are affecting your life until you see them. The top-down process can help you organize and narrow down your search for patterns so that you can focus on where to look for them. In using a top-down approach, you will take what we already know about patterns and apply it to your own life.

Just like the CDC researchers who use the "germ theory of disease" to pinpoint their research, you can use the "pattern theory of being held back from your goals" to focus on the area of your life in which a pattern may be hiding.

What we already know about patterns so far is that they live in the unconscious mind, so we can't readily see them. But we can see the effects of our unproductive patterns in the unfulfilled areas of our lives. Even if we can't immediately see our patterns, we can make a pretty good guess as to where in our lives they are having an impact. Consider this simple question: What area of your life is less than it should be?

In order to use the top-down approach you will have to

take an inventory of your life. Is the underfulfilled area your career, your love life, your health, your family life, your friendships, your finances, your lifestyle, or somewhere else?

Perhaps you may notice that your career is satisfying and you have a great group of friends, but something is amiss in your love life. Probably you have tried to explain this discrepancy to yourself in many ways—bad luck, wrong choices, not the right time for you, too many stresses, career priorities, or those ten extra pounds. Settling on any of these explanations, or being willing to proceed without any explanation at all, is not a very scientific approach to examining your life.

But if, instead, you apply the basic premise of this book—that patterns are likely to be responsible for underachievement—you can therefore make a scientific, top-down assumption that your love life is the area in which an unproductive pattern is most likely to be found. Once you identify the area of your life in which to hunt, you must continue to use a scientific eye, not a fatalistic one, to *see* your pattern clearly.

Discovering Your Pattern from the Bottom Up

Once you identify the general area in which to look for clues, then it is time to start to gather facts and information within that underfulfilled area of your life. You'll need to find out all the details of your unproductive pattern. And that is where the bottom-up approach comes in. And, just like the CDC researchers, you can investigate all the details of the pinpointed area of your life in order to discover the connection between all the facts.

The bottom-up method of study starts by looking at the clues and facts you've gathered to see what conclusions you can draw about the details of your pattern. If working top down tells you in what river to pan for gold, the change to bottom up is the panning process. Bottom-up investigating sifts through all the facts of the spot in your life where you experience underfulfillment.

In using the bottom-up process, you begin by looking at some of the data that you see around you; you look at the nitty-gritty details that you might not previously have considered very important. Often the key to seeing your pattern is hidden in these details.

Some of my patients have told me that the phrase "look into the nitty-gritty details" is my "mantra." And, I do emphasize that phrase. By evaluating the data from these details, you can make some logical conclusions about what the data mean and arrive at some true understanding.

To demonstrate, let's look further into the example where we imagined that your love life has been pinpointed by the top-down method as having less fulfillment than all the other areas of your life. To conduct a bottom-up review of this area, it would make sense that you conduct a careful study of the nitty-gritty facts of your love life in the search for a common thread, a relationship between the facts of your love life and your underfulfillment.

Say you do this for a while, and your research tells you that your love relationships tend to become rocky at the juncture between being uncommitted and becoming committed and exclusive. In that case, you have further zeroed-in on where to look for your pattern. Just by applying these simple steps, you are hot on the pattern's trail. But your fact-finding doesn't end there. Now you can begin studying each situation that takes place around that juncture between non-commitment and commitment.

Let's say that at this juncture you notice that you start to feel uncomfortable with how decisions are made. Maybe you are torn between imposing your will and being accommodating to the wishes of your partner. Maybe you become too dependent and act as if you need the other person more than he or she needs you. Maybe you notice that you become more argumentative to try to stand up for yourself at that point, so you don't "lose yourself."

Or, maybe you observe that you do "lose yourself," that you don't take care of your own needs while catering to another person. Maybe upon investigating further, you notice that you picked people who walked all over you, ordered for you at restaurants, or always selected the movies to see. Or that you picked people who withdrew from you when you needed them, stopped listening to you, or made you feel like a low priority.

Gather the facts. What you discover by using the bottom-up method will help you construct a detailed picture of the action steps that comprise your unproductive pattern. This will help you to connect the dots! Now you have the chance to see your own participation in the pattern that is holding you back—possibly for the first time in your life.

CHAPTER 7

Become a
Pattern Detective

❧

NOW YOU SEE it, now you don't. Some unproductive patterns just jump out at you once you begin to apply scientific observation to your life, but others remain mysterious. You'll have to search for those hard-to-see patterns for a while before they begin to come clear.

In either case, whether a pattern is easy to find or hard to find, the top-down and bottom-up approaches to seeing your patterns are your best tools for discovering them. You have to see your unproductive pattern before you can apply the rest of the SUBGAP method and break it. So, there is no glossing over this step. If at first you don't succeed at *seeing*, keep at it, don't give up. Give yourself some time to apply a scientific eye to your life; the results will be well worth it.

If you are focused on the right area of your life and you

are collecting and digging through all the details of that area—your pattern can't keep hiding. Keep at it and you will find your unproductive pattern. If it is easy to see, you'll find it fast. If it is less apparent, you'll have to roll up your sleeves and get down to examining every nitty-gritty little detail. Like reading a mystery novel, you have to go at your own comfortable pace. You'll find out "whodunit" when you get to the end. During this step, everyone will have his or her own preferred pace. You may work on *seeing* for a while, then put it aside and let what you've discovered already percolate a little, then pick up the search again and look for more clues.

Perhaps you will hit upon your pattern while reading this chapter. Or maybe it will become clear to you as you read the rest of this book. You could figure out your pattern two weeks after you finish this book, or you may have to mull it over, on and off over the coming weeks or months. It may come to you while you are driving to work, or in a conversation with a friend, or while you are on the treadmill or it may hit you like a lightening bolt in the middle of the night, or when you least expect to see it. Your pattern may be blurry at first and become increasingly clear as you continue to zero in.

The important thing to remember is that no pattern can escape this kind of scrutiny. Have confidence that you will achieve the payoff for your detective efforts and that your pattern will be found. Now let's look at some examples of people who learned to see their patterns using the scientific top-down and bottom-up approach.

A Pattern You Can See Quickly: Case of the Violin and the Mack Truck

Let's look at the case of Maria. When Maria came to talk to me, she was in terrible shape. This petite, curly-haired optometrist began to sob as she explained her situation. Haunted by insomnia, she had begun taking sleeping pills. The medicine worked for a while—but when its effect diminished, she had felt she had two alternatives: either take higher doses or switch to different pills. Neither alternative attracted her.

Maria stopped taking the pills without asking her doctor. And things quickly went from bad to worse. She had scarcely slept in days. She reported that she was typically a frazzled person, but now she was even more frazzled and on edge than usual. She couldn't concentrate at work and felt incapable of performing even the simplest eye exam. And that is when she came to talk to me.

She worked in two different offices, one in an eyeglass shop and another in a medical building in which she rented part-time office space from another optometrist. Maria was engaged, and she felt pressured to keep up her earning power. She and her fiancé agreed that they would need to continue to split expenses fifty-fifty after their marriage.

In addition to all the work she was doing, Maria was taking two classes about eye disease to improve her knowledge and be of greater help to her clients. To top it off, she was in the full throes of planning her wedding, with the help of her mother.

The wedding was scheduled to take place back in her home town of Winnipeg, Canada. As a necessary part of wedding preparations, she found herself making regular trips back and forth between Philadelphia and Winnipeg.

Maria was experiencing the stressful negative consequences of an unproductive pattern. While she was well aware of the consequences of it, she could not see the pattern itself. Between her two offices, her two classes, her wedding plans, her awful insomnia, frequent travel to Canada, and financial pressure, the amount of stress she was experiencing was simply too much for her system to bear and she was on overload.

Overexertion took a toll on her immune system, too. She endured a never-ending upper respiratory infection. And even in this state of overdrive, she said that she felt that she was being "a slacker" when she couldn't keep up.

The general outline of Maria's pattern wasn't very hard for her to see. Indeed, when she added up all the facts it was quite obvious—she saw that she was overdoing it. Big time!

But how did she go from being stressed out and thinking only of how to hold herself together, to a point where she could take a scientific look at her life and admit she was overextending herself. In Maria's case, she had to hit rock bottom first. Let's follow her investigation and see.

Getting to the Nitty-Gritty

To discover her pattern, Maria began using the SUBGAP method and first took the "top-down" approach to *seeing*.

When Maria tried to pinpoint the area of her life in which her unproductive pattern was likely to be found, she noted that every area of her life was affected. And this made her feel hopeless about ever seeing her pattern. How could she find the place to start looking for her pattern if every area was affected? But if every area of your life is affected by your pattern, then the pattern is one that impacts something central to your overall health and happiness.

It is not rocket science to determine that Maria's pattern was evident in her approach to many tasks, responsibilities, or decision-making processes. Clearly, she drove herself, and criticized herself when she couldn't keep up the pace. Maria's pattern was to push herself past her healthy limits. Her pattern was in the area of her ability to balance her life and duties, and maintain her physical and emotional health.

Still, Maria had a different idea. She thought she was

going to hunt for a pattern that explained why she was so lazy and hoped that breaking that pattern would allow her to push herself even harder. This was a notion that she would soon discover was false, and furthermore, she would see that calling herself "lazy" was just part of her pattern.

To gather evidence of her pattern, Maria conducted a "bottom-up" investigation of her approach to all the tasks she had taken upon herself. As we now know, the key to the bottom-up approach was to examine all the nitty-gritty details that contributed to her pressure to overdo.

When Maria reflected on her earlier years, she realized that such a pressure-filled attitude toward herself had been her style since her teens. In researching the details of her life, she discovered another area besides sleep was out of balance: that if she didn't eat properly, or often enough, her moods were unstable. But she didn't take the time to eat properly and just kept going. Was her blood sugar affected by her irregular eating patterns? It certainly could have been a factor. It seemed pretty clear that Maria was the kind of person whose equilibrium could be easily thrown out of balance.

The picture, then, was far different from the one Maria had imagined. She wanted to discover that she was a hard-driving, can-do, capable, tough woman who could take everything in stride and was just being lazy. She wanted to discover that she had been right all along to push herself and that all she needed to do was find a way to push herself more. Instead, it became pretty clear to Maria that she was a sensitive person who required careful handling to be happy and healthy.

By talking to me, putting these thoughts into words, and closely examining her life and lifestyle, Maria became aware of the rather finely tuned person she had always been. This was the reality against which she had fought to create a totally different image by acting as if she were a very strong and tough person. This was her pattern, and it was certainly unproductive. It was leading to a total meltdown.

Undeniable Proof

I asked Maria, "If a Mack truck bumps into a guardrail, what happens to the truck?"

"Not much," she answered.

Then I asked, "If a delicate and finely tuned Stradivarius violin bumps into the same guardrail, what happens?"

"It gets destroyed!" Maria replied.

Suddenly her expression changed. "I'm treating myself like I'm a Mack truck right now, aren't I?"

For the first time in her life, Maria saw her pattern as it was occurring. Why hadn't she been able to see it before?

No matter how obvious or simple a pattern is, unless you are looking for it, you are not likely to find it. And unless you are applying the top-down and bottom-up methods of analysis to your own life, the exact details of your pattern may not become clear even if you get to know the general outlines.

When Maria really examined the nitty-gritty details of her pattern, she saw many ways in which it had a negative impact on her well-being. Considering herself lazy, she had been doing all kinds of things to fight her self-perceived laziness. Drinking too much coffee was part of the pattern. So were the sleeping pills, bad eating habits, and insomnia. Feeling frazzled, exhausted, and at her wits' end all were signs of her pattern's activity.

The goal of Maria's pattern was to try to accomplish as much as possible. And Maria's goal was to do the same. Maria's pattern and Maria were in agreement about this much. Getting a lot accomplished is certainly not a bad goal for anyone to have.

So why did things go wrong? They went wrong because Maria's pattern forced her to try to accomplish the goal by pushing herself with no regard for her physical and emotional limits or her personal well-being. Maria's pattern was associated with the idea that she was superwoman and was just being lazy if she couldn't succeed at keeping all the balls in the air. The consequences were serious. And, although the goal was to accomplish more, her pattern made her accomplish *less*. What brought her to grief were the pattern-driven methods she employed to reach her goals.

The question therefore became, how could Maria reach those goals in a manner respectful of her own well-being?

Patterns Make You
a Square Peg in a Round Hole

If you try to fit a square peg into a round hole long enough or forcefully enough, you are going to make that peg pretty miserable. As Maria's plight made so clear, unproductive patterns may be trying to make you into someone you are *not,* instead of helping you to be the best version of who you *are.*

Maria's pattern might have suited someone else, but not her. As she began to recognize that simple fact, for the first time in her life she could consider moving forward and endeavoring to break her old pattern. For, now, she was truly able to *see* it.

Most of the time, finding patterns does take a lot of detective work. Some take more detective work, some take less. Maria's pattern was on the easy side; the facts spoke for themselves. Now let's look at a pattern that took a bit more digging to discover.

Digging Deeper to See a Pattern:
Case of the Cutting Connection

Dahlia came to see me when she was a college senior. She had been cutting herself. Every few weeks, Dahlia made small cuts in her arms and legs using an arts-and-crafts razor knife. Had someone not noticed and urged her to seek help, she might never have thought of this as any great problem. Dahlia admitted that she often felt unhappy but didn't see any connection between her cutting and her unhappiness.

Even when she came to me at the urging of her friends and family, she did not take their worries very seriously. Although she did choose to cut on the inside on her calf and forearms—close to her arteries—Dahlia told me that she was always very careful to avoid cutting into an artery and was highly unlikely to accidentally kill herself this way.

She reported that she simply saw her cutting as a stress release, similar to, say, jogging or yoga. To Dahlia, cutting herself was a *solution* rather than a problem. She could acknowledge that she was generally unhappy. But without her family's urging, it never would have occurred to her to come and talk with me (or anyone else) about her unhappiness. Dahlia did not believe that there was anything she could change or control, and that she simply had to follow along in the same cycle of unhappiness and cutting for relief. She was very fatalistic about it all.

Reluctantly, and only in order to help her family and friends to feel better, Dahlia began to use the SUBGAP method. As Dahlia started to look at her life with a more scientific eye, she actually became excited about the detective work of pattern-hunting.

In our talks I presented the idea that there might be an unproductive pattern somewhere in her life that could be responsible for both the general unhappiness she felt, and for the cutting she used as a relief.

But even as Dahlia became open to the basic concept that an unproductive pattern might be behind both her unhappiness and her self-injury, it was hard for her to determine where her unproductive pattern was hidden. When she tried to apply a top-down approach, all she kept coming up with was that she was generally unhappy with herself. And she had a lot of complaints about how she handled a whole variety of situations.

Some people can see an unproductive pattern in their relationships with others, or in their ability to take care of their health, or in their approach to tasks, or in their pursuit of career goals, or in their ability to balance their pushing and resting (as we saw in Maria's case). For Dahlia, who as we'll soon see was successful in many ways, her focus kept coming back to the one area of her life in which she was underfulfilling her potential.

Since Dahlia was cutting herself not others, kept criticizing herself, and reported being generally unhappy with herself—the area of her life most likely to contain her pattern was her relationship with herself. And that was the place she had to look for the nitty-gritty details.

Words with Herself

Dahlia was a dean's list accounting major whose professors had been encouraging her to go on to get a master's in business administration after she graduated. She looked like the perfect student. She hid her cutting by wearing long-sleeved blouses and sweaters, and long pants.

No one knew how unhappy she felt inside, but she knew, and now she wanted to find out the pattern responsible for her pervasive lack of satisfaction with herself.

Dahlia's bottom-up investigation repeatedly came up with evidence of a very important detail. She discovered that she had an ongoing inner dialogue. Many times a day, she carried on discussions in her head regarding what to do about many situations. She kept all of her inner dialogue to herself. The gist of this inner dialogue consisted of her trying to work out situations by contorting her behavior to fit the situation. And as she further examined her thoughts, she saw that her pattern's strait-jacketing effect upon her true wishes made her very, very uncomfortable.

With that insight, she was now able to focus on the exact area of her relationship with herself that mattered in her unproductive pattern. Dahlia's pattern would reveal itself every time her inner dialogue told her to bend herself out of shape to accommodate others. Repeated detailed examination of events in her daily life led to this conclusion.

Dahlia discovered that during these inner dialogues, she

would begin to feel guilty. Often, she talked herself into taking the blame for anything that went wrong, whether it was truly her fault or not. That was the first hint of a pattern— where she was frequently second-guessing herself, discounting her own opinions, and convincing herself that other people were right and she was wrong.

But, how did her cutting herself figure into this pattern? She had to investigate further.

Making the "Cutting Connection"

While investigating the details of her relationship with herself, Dahlia took a look at her relationship with her boyfriend. There, she found many examples of how she would go against her own interests "to help him." It started to become clear that she felt very guilty and overly responsible toward him, as if he were a helpless baby.

For example, Dahlia got a summer internship in Washington, D.C., in the office of a prestigious consulting firm. The same summer, her boyfriend obtained a similar job in a small accounting firm in Baltimore. When his car broke down, he said he didn't have funds to repair it. So, Dahlia made the long commute to Baltimore whenever he wanted to meet.

She was particularly unhappy that summer. As Dahlia counted all the trips she had made over the past months, she realized she had never concerned herself with whether *she* wanted to meet at the times when her boyfriend did.

In her bottom-up examination of the details of those trips, Dahlia noticed that, whenever she got home from visiting her boyfriend, she mentally kicked herself for having made the effort to see him. But then, she immediately chided herself in her inner dialogue for having any resentment. How could she question the worth of making him happy? Why should she feel so burdened by him? These kinds of reactions made her feel extremely uncomfortable.

In the midst of all these conflicting inner arguments and emotions—Dahlia found that cutting herself made her feel better and more relaxed. After she cut herself, she could put the issue to rest and not think about it again until she returned home from the next visit.

Finally, the cutting connection became clear. As soon as she began cutting herself, her guilt went away. The focus on that self-injuring action distracted her attention away from her feelings of being upset. Instead of doing anything constructive to either solve the problem directly with the boyfriend or reevaluate her relationship with him, she simply punished herself for any conflict she had while complying with his wishes.

The cutting made the issue go away—for a short while at least. By making the issue go away temporarily, the cutting also guaranteed that the pattern would continue and the issue would return.

Encouraged by what she was learning about herself, Dahlia began keeping a journal. There, she recorded her inner dialogue. All the decision-making that related to her boyfriend and others was put into words.

As she continued to study her pattern, her journal-keeping became easier. She was able to relate the details that led up to each event of upset and cutting. It became clear that each time there was an episode, it was preceded by a justifiable, normal, healthy feeling that her cutting wiped away. By wiping the feeling away, her pattern continued, and her life remained unhappy.

Dahlia began to understand that issues needed to be addressed and resolved instead of temporarily quelled by cutting. The important thing was, she had already accomplished the first step—*seeing*. As it is for many people, *seeing* was far more difficult than she had imagined it would be, in part because the pattern was so deeply hidden. But, once she saw her pattern, Dahlia's whole perspective on her life was transformed. She now had a chance of being happier. She was on her way to the next steps of the SUBGAP method.

For the Record

Another key to applying the scientific approach to your own life is putting what you see into words. When you do, it gives you more power over the thing you see. Putting an identifying label on something that you couldn't see before is a very empowering action. It gives you a shorthand that makes the rest of the pattern-breaking steps in the SUBGAP method go more smoothly.

You may find yourself saying, "There I go, putting the cart before the horse again," or "There I go, wearing my heart on my sleeve again," or "There I go not speaking up for myself again," or whatever your unproductive pattern entails. But seeing it and labeling it brings the pattern out of the shadows and into the light of scientific scrutiny, where it can be broken.

It was Freud's belief that the most valid way to put your findings into words was to tell them to your psychoanalyst, as we saw Maria do earlier in this chapter. But it's my view that there are other effective ways to put your findings into words—ways that don't require getting on the analytic couch. Self-talk silently to yourself or actually talking aloud, can help in defining what it is that you see about yourself. Or you can keep a journal, as we just saw Dahlia do. You can write about what you see and the clues you gather, or write a story about it, or a poem. Still another way is to include friends or family members in your hunt for your clues and keep them informed about it.

Or, if you typically talk to yourself through a form of creativity other than words, you can even express what you find out through other modes. You might choreograph a dance to it, compose a song about it, or make it the theme of a painting or sculpture. If words are not your forte, expressing what you have learned about your pattern through your art or music will still give you extra power in the process of exploration.

Before you can do anything about your unproductive pattern, you have to *see* it and be able to describe it. Then you have more power to *do* something about it—and you can begin to *gain mastery over the pattern that had mastery over you!*

CHAPTER 8

Your Dignity Shield

❧

AS WE DISCOVERED in the last chapter, learning to see your unproductive pattern is sometimes easy and sometimes difficult. It requires a scientific approach. But, in addition to the top-down and bottom-up approaches, there is one more key issue related to *seeing*. *In learning to see your pattern, sometimes the most difficult thing is learning to stop "not-seeing" your patterns.*

We human beings are dignified creatures, but sometimes our dignity works against us. We take ourselves very seriously and are sometimes too hard on ourselves. Our "Dignity Shield," as I call it, keeps us from noticing our mistakes because we don't want to think of ourselves as heading down the wrong path. We don't want to feel silly.

Our Dignity Shield is the part of us that prefers to keep

patterns hidden. You're probably familiar with that part of yourself. It's the voice that says "Don't rock the boat!" It's the part of us that finds comfort in the status quo; no matter what the consequences of the status quo. If we don't see our patterns we don't have to feel that we have been doing the wrong thing. That way we won't be hard on ourselves. But, sometimes you have to give yourself permission to be human, and admit to some mistakes to be able to see your pattern.

Self-Protection

The Dignity Shield might lead us to overlook evidence of participating in an unproductive pattern, since dignified people never want to view themselves as foolish or wrong-minded. Unacknowledged, then, the pattern can keep operating in secret. Given the protection of our Dignity Shield—keeping mistakes under wraps—we don't correct ourselves. Therefore, the unproductive pattern can maintain control over us.

One of the secrets of patterns, as we've seen in earlier chapters, is that they're based upon optimistic motives. It's optimistic energy that compels you to repeat your pattern in the hope that if you repeat your pattern often enough, one of those times, maybe the next time, it will get you the desired outcome. The optimistic feeling while repeating a pattern is almost addictive, blinding us to the fact that the pattern has failed before and is ultimately going to hold us back again.

That's why people will so often maintain a pattern even when it's clearly taking them on a detour away from goals. Caught up in the momentum of optimism, we enjoy the feeling that we are on the road to success or happiness even when the pattern is actually taking us on a wild-goose chase.

Patterns, after all, are formed by series of steps. The path becomes familiar. Whether they're real steps forward, or just missteps, they feel just as good while we are traveling them because we're walking a well-worn pathway. We feel, "At least we are doing something, at least we are trying." We feel uplifted by hope of success as we continue on our way. Until, of course, the unproductiveness of the pattern foils us in the end, opportunities are lost, and we are back to square one.

Becoming consciously aware of your real situation, patterns and all, is the best chance you have for success. But what you discover about yourself may sting. It's no fun finding out that you've been wasting time and energy going after your goals the wrong way for a long time. Can you stand a little pinch in your pride? As Dr. Suyin Han said, "Truth, like surgery, may hurt, but it cures."

Are you willing to see your pattern even if it makes you feel a bit silly at first? Are you willing to find out that you have been heading down the wrong path without even knowing it?

"My Name is _____, and I Am a Pattern-a-holic"

In Alcoholics Anonymous, the first step to recovery is to admit that you have a problem with alcohol. Far more of us are members of *Pattern-a-holics Anonymous,* where it's sometimes just as tough to admit that you have a pattern problem. Everyone who is underachieving or underfulfilled—and there are millions of us—has to take the first step and admit to having unproductive patterns.

Admitting to unproductive patterns certainly doesn't mean you should think badly of yourself or blame yourself. Getting out the cat-o'-nine-tails and emotionally whipping yourself for having participated in a pattern is not any more productive than having participated in the pattern in the first place. Okay, even if things have not, to date, worked out as you'd like in a certain area of your life, that's no reason to be hard on yourself. It's not your fault. You probably didn't even know about your pattern, since it lived in your unconscious mind. It just means you need to admit a few things—that you have a pattern that is preventing you from doing the best thing for yourself. Once that admission is made, learning can begin. You can apply the SUBGAP method, break the pattern, and improve.

Don't waste your energy on mea culpas. Patterns develop through no fault of your own. They are the result of a confluence of factors, and there are ways to understand how these patterns have developed, as I'll discuss that more in the next chapter. The good news is that even though you didn't choose to have an unproductive pattern, you can choose to be rid of it. In short, a key element in the *seeing* process is *choosing to see*.

"His and Her" Dignity Shields

In relationships, and especially in a marriage, the Dignity Shield that I have described often comes in the plural form. Two people, two patterns, two Dignity Shields. This was certainly the case in the following example of Irene and Alan.

Alan and Irene were a dual-career couple with three kids. In their twelve years of marriage, Irene and Alan had become mutual participants in a pattern that worsened over the years and made both of them miserable.

Their pattern only showed itself when the two of them disagreed or their needs did not coincide. However, with time, their disagreements became more frequent. They disagreed about very important issues, such as how to raise their children and what to do in the bedroom. They also disagreed about seemingly minor issues, such as where to have dinner. In each of these situations Alan would loudly declare his position, and Irene would immediately tell her husband to "just do whatever *you* want to do." Almost invariably, the disagreement would end with her declaring, "I just don't care anymore."

Yet each time Irene gave in, she felt Alan had dominated her. She felt unwillingly forced to follow his dictates. On

Alan's part, when his wife gave in, he accepted her words at face value. Since he was unaware that he had raised his voice, all he saw was that Irene told him to do what he wanted. So, he proceeded to do just that.

Even in a situation where Irene voiced a mild objection the first time, he simply pressed the issue again, and she would inevitably fold. So as far as Alan was concerned, things were fine. He certainly couldn't imagine that he was doing anything that could be seen as inconsiderate. It never occurred to him that he might drive away his wife through these actions.

Finally after years of this pattern, Irene became sullen and depressed and contemplated divorce. At this point, they came in to see me as a couple.

Now You See It, Now You Don't

As Alan talked about himself, it didn't take long to learn some of the background of his part in the couple's pattern. He had grown up in a household where all the children were spoiled. He discovered quickly that by repeatedly insisting or by raising his volume he would get what he wanted, so those were the methods of persuasion he learned to use.

Irene, on the other hand, grew up in a household where her father ruled with an iron hand. His word was law, and his rebukes were barbed and painful punishment.

And now, both of them were playing out the patterns from their childhoods in every "he said—she said" report of conflict. I started asking Alan if he noticed that Irene became withdrawn every time he interrupted her. Right at the moment I pointed it out, Alan seemed to notice what he was doing, and he would hold himself back for a few seconds. Once or twice, he openly admitted that he had completely tuned out what Irene had said. And, in what seemed like a breakthrough, Alan even expressed his willingness to relisten to his wife's point of view. It seemed that he was on the verge of seeing that he might be playing a role in the couple's pattern.

Turning to Irene, I explained that her husband finally seemed willing to listen to her point of view and asked her if she'd like to restate her point. If she stuck to her guns and stated her viewpoint, and if he really listened, it would have been a first for both of them. Indeed, that exchange might have been a watershed moment in their marriage.

Instead, when Alan was momentarily ripe for listening, Irene told him it didn't matter any more whether she had a chance to be heard or not. She then encouraged him—as usual—to go on with whatever point he was trying to make when he first interrupted her, and so he did.

Right there, in that exchange, was a good example of the "now you see it, now you don't" aspect of patterns. The Dignity Shield might lower for a minute. But all too quickly, it lifts back up. The protective armor is in place again. The couple's moment for *seeing* was gone, and the pattern continued throughout that session and the next ones.

Shields Up!

In defense of his dignity, Alan offered ample "proof" of how considerate he could be. He talked about running errands and cooking for the family. He felt he was being the best father and husband he knew how. But he overlooked his walking all over Irene's wishes. In fact, except for this domineering and inconsiderate streak, he was a good and responsible man.

Irene was also a responsible, good parent, and a steady partner. Even while Alan had been through a series of trials and tribulations with his business, she had held firm. She felt that she was much more mature because she never had a tantrum, never raised her voice or demanded her way. Comparing her husband's behavior to her own, Irene viewed him as immature. She blamed Alan for all the problems in their relationship. "He's the wrong type of man for me," she said more than once. "I'm a healthy person! I deserve better."

Clearly, it was a difficult situation. Irene and Alan each needed to feel they had done nothing wrong. So there was no option but to feel that any problem was all the other person's fault. Their Dignity Shields cancelled out the opportunity to see the unproductive pattern in which they *both* participated, and eliminated the opportunity to change it.

The truth is, no matter how much we admit that we are not perfect, there is something about the reality of seeing our imperfections that backs us into a corner. We want to say, "It's not so!"

The natural, human response is to hold up the Dignity Shield for protection. That's what Alan and Irene were doing. Neither of them could let their shields down. They didn't or couldn't see their patterns. Under the circumstances, the pinch to their pride would have been more than either were willing or able to tolerate.

The result was sad and difficult for both of them. Their marriage ended.

Become a Bigger Person

Seeing your patterns means you have to stretch. You have to become a slightly bigger person than you are now. Not a whole lot bigger—just big enough to notice that, in participating in your pattern, you are doing something that is contributing to your underfulfillment.

Often, the ability to see your own pattern requires some swallowing of pride. There is good news and bad news in this requirement. The bad news, of course, is that you will probably find out you have been participating in a series of action steps that add up to an unproductive pattern. And there will be a little pinch in your dignity when you admit this. But don't forget the good news. If, indeed, you can accept that you have a pattern that is holding you back, you can learn to break it.

It is within your power to stop the pattern precisely because you are the one who participates in it. If the "command central" of your actions is not fate or bad luck or the actions of others—that means *you have more power than you think you do.*

Swallowing Pride for Love

On the bright side, there are numerous cases in which people have applied the SUBGAP method and found themselves willing to swallow their pride to achieve their goals. One person who comes to mind as an example is Stephanie, a woman I met when she was in her late fifties, soon after she had been fortunate enough to retire early from her career as a stockbroker. She moved near the water, to a small town near Puget Sound, in Washington, where she could enjoy nature and the wonderful scenery.

For years before retirement, she had been looking forward eagerly to the time she would have for enjoyment. She anticipated the days when she would have time for her hobbies, and be free to enjoy visiting with her daughter and grandchildren.

The Very Empty Nest

After three years of retirement during which Stephanie extended numerous invitations to her daughter and grandchildren, she had not been rewarded with a single visit. As a matter of fact, Stephanie's daughter, Eleanor, usually ignored Stephanie's invitations completely.

At first, Stephanie thought the problem might be money, so she offered to pay for the trip. Her daughter made excuses that were obviously intended to put her off.

Stephanie still couldn't figure it out. Maybe the problem was bad timing. Instead of inviting her daughter for holidays, she extended open invitations. Still, she saw no results. She was offering a beautiful environment, a great place for grandchildren to play, and an invitation to visit anytime— what was the matter? Stephanie finally asked her daughter if there was anything wrong.

She was met with a brick wall. Eleanor denied any problem. She was simply very busy. That was that.

And visits weren't the only problem. Last October, Stephanie called Eleanor and asked what her two young grandsons wanted for Christmas. Eleanor didn't know. She said she'd find out. Two weeks later, Stephanie called again. Had the boys made up their minds yet?

"Sorry," said Eleanor, they hadn't discussed it. She would talk to them and get back to her mother.

By November, Stephanie still had not received a reply, so she sent the kids gift certificates to a sporting goods store in their neighborhood. When the holiday season passed, and the new year brought no further word from her daughter or grandsons, Stephanie called Eleanor and asked if the boys had received their presents. Her daughter replied that they had. Stephanie could contain herself no longer.

"Well, an acknowledgment would have been appreciated!" she told her daughter. "Believe me, when someone sends me a present, I *always* thank the person in a timely manner."

The call ended on a bad note, and afterward, Stephanie found it increasingly difficult to get through. For the next three months, though Stephanie left messages, Eleanor did not reply to her calls.

"What did I do to deserve this?" Stephanie wondered aloud when she met with me, "I think I was a good mother!" It didn't take very much top-down analysis to see that Eleanor and the grandchildren were what was missing from Stephanie's dream of retirement.

Yes, Stephanie admitted, her brief lecture on acknowledging the presents was probably hard for Eleanor to take. "But was it really so bad that she would want to avoid her for months afterward, or did it run deeper than that?"

She was clearly bothered by Eleanor's rejection of her and I helped her to embark on a bottom-up investigation to find out exactly what made her daughter so touchy. Stephanie didn't think that she had ever done anything to deserve such rejection, but, as opposed to the couple in our previous example, she seemed open to finding out the real reasons.

Whose Life Is It Anyway?

A nitty-gritty review of their history showed that Stephanie and her daughter had been growing apart since Eleanor was in high school. Stephanie didn't try to hide any of the facts from herself or from me, and reported candidly that a key point of conflict had been over the question of whether Eleanor should have breast-reduction surgery. At the time, Stephanie felt very strongly that her daughter's breasts were too heavy and that they would make Eleanor physically uncomfortable. Eleanor, however, was undecided and didn't want to discuss it. She had resented her mother's insistent suggestions, and did everything she could to avoid the topic.

Nor was that the only point of contention. Stephanie did her best to remember and report on incident after incident. Between Stephanie and Eleanor, it was clear, there existed a long history of episodes where Stephanie had made well-intentioned suggestions that Eleanor regarded as overly critical or controlling. As Stephanie talked about these episodes, the relationship damaging pattern took shape. Numerous times, Stephanie tried to "help" her daughter with "little suggestions" about Eleanor's appearance, clothes, education, and more recently about the raising of the two boys.

Could Stephanie's unsolicited suggestions have been interpreted as criticism? Could her attempts to help have been seen as attempts to control? In reviewing all the details, Stephanie had to admit that these conclusions were possible, even though she believed that she was doing the right thing each time by making suggestions to help her daughter.

Stephanie never got the hint, until she applied a scientific eye to the details of this area of underfulfillment. It was a leap for Stephanie to *see* this pattern. But when she did see it, she was nearly heartbroken by what she observed in her past pattern of behavior and its effect upon Eleanor. She loved her daughter deeply. She never intended to criticize Evelyn, much less make her feel hurt.

Stephanie was particularly disappointed in herself because, having been raised by a very critical mother herself, she had vowed never to repeat that pattern with her own children.

The Pattern Stops Here

Yes, the pattern went back through the generations. She recalled how her mother had constantly pointed out that Stephanie was overweight. Stephanie's mother had monitored every meal, counted every morsel of food to "help"

Stephanie "not go through life as a fat girl." Stephanie was well aware of the pain that such comments had caused her.

But in some ways her memory of that embarrassment was a help to her. Because, now, she was ready to learn more about her own pattern, to understand it and to break it for the good of her daughter and their relationship.

It takes a big person to admit having made a single mistake that he or she wasn't aware of making. It takes an *even bigger* person to admit that he or she has been making those mistakes every day—possibly for years and years. Going one step further, it takes great strength of character to go *looking* to find the patterns that are contributing to those mistakes.

It was something that Stephanie was ultimately able to do. She suffered the pinch to her dignity and moved on. Her motivation was strong. After all, this was something she would have to deal with if she and her daughter were going to come to terms with their relationship. And that motivation helped push Stephanie to become more aware of the mistakes she had been making and the choices that she faced in the future.

If you are motivated to make things better for youself and those you love, you *can* become a bigger person. You can push past your Dignity Shield and see your patterns. Now, the next step in the SUBGAP method is to *understand* what you see.

PART THREE

Understanding

⁓

The highest activity a human being can attain
is learning for understanding,
because to understand is to be free.
—Benedict de Spinoza

CHAPTER 9

The Power of Understanding

~

ONCE YOU ARE able to *see* your pattern and put it into words, the next step is to *understand* your pattern. This is the second part of the SUBGAP method.

Understanding your patterns will have several powerful and life-altering effects upon you. It will prepare you, motivate you, and give you the right perspective to do battle with your patterns and break them.

What's to Understand?

Exactly what can you understand when you understand your pattern?

- You can understand exactly how your pattern operates

in your daily life, precisely how it holds you back, and what you are missing out on as a result.

- You can understand how events in your life have shaped your patterned behavior, and you can better evaluate when you are being controlled by your past.

- You can understand what motivates your pattern and what participating in your pattern aims to achieve, and you can compare those goals to the ones that you truly want for yourself.

- You can understand that you still have the potential to be more fulfilled and successful, that your pattern never took this away from you, and that you can break your pattern and move ahead.

- You can understand that the unpleasant feelings that come along with missing out, such as disappointment in yourself or feeling stuck, are really a reflection of your pattern's effect upon your life *and not a reflection on you* or your potential. You can understand that these unpleasant feelings are not a permanent condition and will go away when you break your pattern and are no longer missing out.

- Most importantly, you can come to understand—with great clarity—that you and your pattern are separate. Even if you've been participating in your pattern for a long time, and even if you've begun doubting your potential to succeed—*you are not your pattern.*

The "Me" and "Not-Me" of Understanding

Understanding patterns helps us to ask questions about the difference between two ways of living—living under the pattern's control and living free of it.

Your identity is impacted by how you live, and what you achieve personally and professionally. If an unproductive pattern is holding you back, your sense of identity will be affected. You will begin to think of yourself as less than you are. Given enough years of participating in a pattern that holds you back, you might find yourself adjusting your identity downward to match the reduced fulfillment in your life.

When you call yourself "me," to whom, exactly, are you referring? Are you referring to the "me" that is the self you feel deep down, the one with all the potential that has yet to be fulfilled? Or are you referring to the "me" that is participating in unproductive patterns and holding you back from success and fulfillment? That pattern-following "me" is the one that is identified with reduced success and limited fulfillment.

You have probably thought about yourself in the same way for a long time, maybe even for most of your life. But, like most people with unproductive patterns, odds are that you are folding your patterns into your view of yourself along with the authentic elements of your personality. This results in a picture of yourself that is all mixed-up with your patterns.

Instead of understanding your patterns, you might be

holding yourself responsible for not reaching your goals, or deciding you are not up to the task in some way. Confusing yourself with your patterns is a *big mistake*. On the other hand, clarifying this confusion validates who you are and points out the nature of the enemy. As I said, you are not your pattern.

You and your pattern may be temporarily sharing the same mind and sharing the same life in the same town, but, as the classic western movie tells us, "This town isn't big enough for the both of us." Your pattern has to go! If you can understand what part of the picture is the real you and what part of the picture is your pattern, you know what to fight and there is no chance that what you will fight is yourself.

Not Feeling Like Yourself?

When your pattern has led you to underachievement or under-fulfillment in certain areas of your life, you get accustomed to feeling a certain way about that underfulfillment and under-achievement. You might attribute this to "the way I usually feel."

For instance, if your pattern has led you to always be a friend and never a romantic interest, you may have come to feel that you are not as desirable as others. If your pattern is broken, and romance can enter your life, that feeling of undesirability would quickly go away. Understanding that the underfulfilled way you may normally feel *is associated with your pattern* means that you recognize the potential for feeling better about yourself and your life. As I'll describe in the case histories in the next two chapters, this kind of emotional understanding provides both a sense of relief and a sense of excitement about future possibility.

There is relief in that you no longer have to hide from the feeling that something is amiss. If you understand that these feelings you've come to know as your "usual feeling" about yourself are instead part of your pattern, you also understand that they are temporary. They are not your permanent feeling of identity. They can go away when your pattern goes away, and you can look forward to feeling better about yourself.

The Inspiration Factor

When you *understand* your pattern, the connection between the pattern and your ability to achieve your potential becomes quite clear. Making this connection gives you inspiration. You can reclaim your dreams.

Remember those? The dreams you put away with the checked baggage at some point?   Reclaim them. Get inspired. When you break the hold that your patterns have upon you, you can move more vigorously toward the life that you feel, deep down, is meant to be.

It is a big step to start to think about your life as having two paths at any moment. When you regard yourself as a combination of the patterned and unpatterned parts, you have already taken a leap in your perspective about yourself. Possibly for the first time in your life, you can reach an understanding and help separate your patterned self from your unpatterned self.

There are two types of understanding that you can apply to your pattern—*historical understanding* and *operational understanding*. Both types help you gain that extra oomph you need to break your pattern. Both help you to develop an understanding of your pattern as separate from yourself. And, as you'll see in the next chapters, either one of these ways of understanding—or even a combination of both—will enhance your ability to become free of your unproductive patterns.

There is the path through your life that *you* would choose for yourself and the path that *your pattern would choose for you.* By understanding your pattern you increase the chances of gaining enough perspective to choose properly each time.

CHAPTER 10

Historical Understanding

THERE IS A Latin expression, *"Qui me amat, amat et canem meam."* It means, essentially, if you love me, you'll love my dog too. The phrase implies that "me and my dog" are a package deal. You don't get one without the other.

When your patterns have been with you a long time, you don't realize that you bring them with you everywhere you go and introduce them to everyone you meet. You could be presenting yourself and your patterns as a package deal without knowing it.

When you can gain a *historical understanding* of patterns, you have a unique opportunity to separate your patterns from your "self." Patterns may be "following you around" like that proverbial dog. They really have very little to do with you, and certainly aren't a part of you. And the fact is, your life is likely to be vastly improved if you can recognize them and leave them behind.

If your unproductive pattern of behavior has been with you so long that you can't tell the difference between yourself and your pattern, a *historical understanding* may clarify this for you.

A *historical understanding* of your patterns entails making the connection between your childhood/teen experiences and the pattern in which you are participating right now. This method is not for everyone. Why? Because not everyone remembers enough of his or her childhood or teen years to apply this method. Besides, not everyone is in the right frame of mind to go rooting around in the past. But for those who are, and for those who have a lot of memories (whether pleasant or unpleasant), this could be the way to proceed.

A Historical Understanding: A Case of Love Me, Love My Dog

To see how you can learn to separate that raggedy old dog of patterns that may have followed you for a while, let's look at the case of Rudy.

Rudy was a painfully shy man who felt he was underachieving in many areas. When he consulted with me, he presented himself as a person who seemed to have everything he needed to be popular. But he was far from that. He was a wallflower. Had that been Rudy's real self—if that was a natural condition for him—he would have been quite comfortable being a wallflower. Instead, Rudy had the feeling he wasn't meant to be a wallflower.

Rudy was a tall, handsome, athletic guy just over forty. As a triathlete, he relished the kind of activity that awed others. He could run for six miles right after biking for twenty-two miles, which, of course, he did immediately after swimming for 1,500 meters.

In addition, Rudy had many hobbies and interests. He played the guitar and regularly joined up with a Celtic music group for "open mike night" in a neighborhood tavern. With all these interests and activities in his life, the contrast with Rudy's "loner" persona was striking. When people talked with him at work, during his sports activities, or even in his music group, his shyness came out. He became tongue-tied and withdrew as quickly as possible.

Needless to say, Rudy's social awkwardness had affected his personal life. He had never married. As a matter of fact, when he came to see me, he hadn't even been on a date in the previous three years. His prior relationships had been brief and had ended in rejection or in his walking away.

Shyness also inhibited his career. While Rudy had worked in a variety of different jobs, primarily in the insurance industry, he reported that the longest he held any one position was about two years.

The Trouble with Rudy

At the time he first consulted with me, Rudy had been working as a claims adjuster for a national insurance company. We talked about a very touchy situation he was in with his boss, the head of the claims department at the local branch. His boss seemed to be getting the impression that Rudy was not able to carry out assignments properly. Rather than wrapping things up quickly, his boss observed, Rudy dragged his feet when he was collecting the facts of any damage or loss investigation.

Rudy's side of the story was different. His boss, he said, was constantly overwhelmed and didn't give him clear instructions or deadlines. Whatever the true story, the facts were that Rudy was in trouble and his boss was unhappy with his performance. As a result, Rudy felt afraid to go into work.

He told me he had recently taken several days off as sick time rather than face the potential conflicts and humiliations that he anticipated if he went in to work. He could feel the tension building, knew that he faced the possibility of being dismissed—unless he quit first.

However precarious things were for Rudy at work, he reported a similarly unstable personal life with many brief relationships that ended in rejection or his running away. Rudy said he felt so nervous about things going wrong that he couldn't even bring himself to date these days.

Is It Me or Them?

Rudy longed for acceptance, but he didn't come to talk with me because he wanted to break his pattern of getting into trouble and running away. Rudy readily saw that there was a pattern *in his life* that led to all his bouncing around from job to job and all his dating troubles. He saw that this pattern made him feel like a failure. But as he saw it, the pattern was due to the fact others didn't accept him, and that, try as he might, he wasn't able to be the kind of person who would be appreciated.

Rudy did not *understand* that the pattern was *his* pattern and that he had the power to change it. He didn't understand that his pattern was stopping him from being the kind of person he imagined he could and should be. An important distinction! It had never occurred to him that the problem could be related to an unproductive pattern *inside of him*. Instead he saw his problems as the result of a lack of understanding by others. From his perspective, he was a victim of a cold world that couldn't accept people with difficulties like his.

I was reminded of the fictional character, Blanche Dubois in the Tennessee Williams play *A Streetcar Named Desire*. Rudy had "always relied on the kindness of strangers." He hoped that others would change their attitudes toward him and make him feel more comfortable. He was relying on others to break the pattern.

A Bundle of Energy

When Rudy consulted with me and began to talk about his life, it was clear he had a very good memory and was able to conjure parts of his past. It quickly became apparent that Rudy would be a likely candidate for discovering a *historical understanding* of his situation.

Rudy reported that, when he was five or six, his parents described him as a "bundle of energy." But it wasn't a bundle they necessarily enjoyed. His mother persuaded Rudy's pediatrician to medicate him with a prescribed tranquilizer. When this did not sedate him enough for everyone's liking, she decided that she couldn't deal with a rambunctious boy like him. Rudy's mother decided to send him to boarding school in another state and his father went along with the idea

Rudy continued in boarding schools, moving from one to another, all the way up until college. With every move, he became progressively more unhappy, and he kept asking his parents to bring him back home and send him to public school. They would not. He came home only for holidays and summers.

Not surprisingly, Rudy blamed himself for being the boy who needed to be medicated and sent away. He concluded that he couldn't be a pleasing enough five-year-old unless he had some sort of medicine to "calm him down." And Rudy's take on the situation was that by the time he was a ten-year-old, he was such a "failure" that he had to be sent away.

His academic history was spotty. Occasionally he got good grades in some areas—then he would move, or change classes, and his performance plummeted. He attended three different colleges before graduating.

All his life after that, and throughout his relationships and work histories, Rudy repeated a pattern of being too impulsive or impatient, getting into trouble, and ending up going away in failure when things got tough.

What's You and What's Not You?

This brings us back to the very important point regarding the "me and not-me" of patterns. That is, after having participated in a pattern for a long time, you get the idea, wrong as it might be, that the pattern *is* you. You start to believe that the pattern is your real self, when it is not.

Once you start to think that the pattern is you, as Rudy had done, if people don't accept your *patterned behavior,* you believe, mistakenly, that they are not accepting *you.* This formula can apply to any way that your life may be falling short of your hopes and dreams. Are *you* falling short, or is your *pattern* holding you back?

Rudy had a lot of strengths, and had the potential to be the people person he always wanted to be—a potential he felt deep down. In point of fact, people never actually got a chance to know Rudy because the pattern got in the way. And to take it one step further—Rudy never even got to *know himself* because the pattern got in the way! But still, he always had a sense that this wasn't the life he was meant to be living.

The world is not a bed of roses. People can be heartless at times. That's not news to anybody. If Rudy's goal was to change the world, and people, in order to get himself accepted (patterned behavior and all), that was most certainly an unrealistic goal. If his patterned goal was to repeat his nervous pattern, and to give people the message that he was halfway out the door at all times—the world was not likely to accept him on those terms.

When Rudy looked at the nitty-gritty details of his present problems at work and socializing side by side with those of his life history, he found more than sufficient evidence to make a connection between the two. The fact that a pattern had formed in the past and was continuing into the present was undeniable. Once he saw this, he couldn't possibly brush off his pattern and shift blame to the world-at-large for mistreating him.

By looking at his history and learning about how his pattern came to be, Rudy now *understood* that participating in this pattern was coming from inside of himself. And having understood that, he was prepared to accept that only he could change it.

Understanding created a shift in his perspective.

The Enemy within Is NOT You

Rudy was quite emotional when he discovered that the pattern was *inside of him*, but was *not him*. He admitted that he had been overlooking the fact that his pattern made him behave like a rambunctious kid who still longed to be accepted, even at the age of forty. "Maybe that acceptance should have happened when I was five or ten, but it didn't."

"I'm still looking to get that acceptance I missed in my childhood," he said, and then corrected himself, "No, *my pattern* is making me look for that acceptance instead of helping myself to have a better life!"

At last, this handsome, intelligent, athletic, talented man realized that he was going to underfulfill his personal and professional potential if he kept participating in this pattern.

Once the historical approach helped Rudy to understand his pattern, he became able to take more careful note of its occurrences. When he got nervous on the job, he noticed that he instantly became "rambunctious." That's when he got tongue-tied and mixed up, forgot important things, made careless mistakes while trying to rush, got into trouble, and felt like a failure.

When Rudy began keeping a journal, he noted how, in social situations, his rambunctious behavior went hand-in-hand with a great fear of rejection. Following my prescription to put his SUBGAP process into words, he began to talk to his friends about his quest to understand his pattern. One friend, when sitting with Rudy after his music night at the pub, made some very candid observations that proved helpful. The friend pointed out that whenever Rudy felt awkward or shy, he fidgeted, talked fast, bit his fingernails, interrupted, and shifted in his seat constantly—not exactly the best behavior for an eligible bachelor trying to put his best foot forward.

Before having understood his pattern, Rudy would never have conceived of asking for this kind of feedback. It would have been impossible for him to accept that portrait of himself, even from someone who had the best of intentions. *But now what he heard was the description of a pattern, not a portrait of who he was.*

This shift was accomplished when Rudy was able to, as he put it, "connect the dots" from his childhood through the present. People could love him, but that didn't mean they had to love his bad behavior. It no longer had to be a package deal. Rudy came to understand that, if he broke his pattern, more people in the world might just have the opportunity to love him for himself.

Now, armed with this understanding, Rudy was ready to apply the next step in the SUBGAP method and work on breaking his pattern for the first time in his life.

Another Historical Approach:
The Case of "Stop Me Before I Help Again!"

Chelsea was a bright and sensible person, except when her pattern made her subject to the whims of those around her. By the time she came to talk with me, her pattern of extending herself for others had really worn her down. It had taken a toll on her immune system. Chelsea was often ill, frequently afflicted with colds and constantly fatigued. Still, she could always be found chauffeuring friends to their appointments, baby-sitting, dog-sitting, errand-running, event-planning, gift-buying, caretaking, covering shifts for co-workers, running fund-raisers for church, money-lending, and lending an ear—no matter whether she had the time, energy, or money to do so.

Chelsea's live-in boyfriend recently had a business setback and was in debt. As a result, she felt under a lot of pressure to earn enough money to support both of them. There were family demands as well. Her mother had recently undergone heart surgery. But instead of going to a hospital near Chelsea, her mom had chosen one that was nearly three hundred miles away. Chelsea commuted every weekend during her mother's long recuperation without saying a word about it.

As she examined the details of her pattern, it became clear to Chelsea that she felt compelled to keep pushing herself. It was also clear that she did so without complaint and never,

ever, said no. Her stress was something she never discussed with her mother or boyfriend. She was convinced that unless she pushed herself, her world would crumble.

To Chelsea, everything that happened and every favor asked of her was at the level of a life-or-death emergency. However minor the situation in another person's eyes, Chelsea treated each task as a mission, putting the same urgent pressure on herself.

One price that Chelsea paid was that she suffered a lot of anxiety. It came welling up when she had to explain herself to someone at work. Even when questioned on relatively unimportant matters, she was always afraid she would get into trouble and be fired, or afraid she'd offend a friend or relative and cause a rift in the relationship and lose the person.

All this was puzzling to her. And there was another factor that just didn't seem to fit at all. Whenever Chelsea heard a police siren or ambulance siren, or saw a police car, her anxiety became almost unbearable. For no good reason—at least none that she could determine—she simply had a great fear of the police. Any encounter of any kind stirred a panic that would last for hours.

Going Back in Time

Over and over again, Chelsea asked, "Why do I drive myself crazy like this?" She just assumed there were no answers and felt fatefully resigned to pushing herself to do the next task.

While Chelsea saw her pattern and recognized that participating in it was hurting her, she couldn't stop herself. Even if it was making her sick, she couldn't put a halt to the pattern. Chelsea's case is a good example to show that *seeing* your unproductive pattern without *understanding* it may not affect your pattern's control over you. The idea of *not pushing* herself made her even more nervous than the idea of continuing to push herself. To achieve an understanding of her pattern—and get the oomph to break it—I encouraged Chelsea to explore her history.

As Chelsea reviewed her life to gain a *historical understanding* of her pattern, her focus returned to one important detail over and over again. When Chelsea was twelve years old, her father had attempted suicide with a handgun. Chelsea was the one who had found him lying on the floor, blood spurting from his chest. It was up to the twelve-year-old girl to call the sheriff's department in her small Texas town. Rushing back to her unconscious father, she put pressure on his wound until the ambulance arrived.

But the nightmare had only begun. The follow-up investigation revealed that Chelsea's father, the bookkeeper for the town's paper mill, had been "cooking the books" for some time. He had skimmed off profits for himself and his family but had gotten caught and was in serious trouble. Rather than face arrest and trial, he had shot himself.

Though Chelsea's father eventually recovered, the disgrace did not go away. Everyone knew what her father had done.

Throughout her father's long hospital stay, during his trial for embezzlement and felony forgery, and during his time in jail, Chelsea and her mother were constant targets of gossip and ill will.

Instead of receiving sympathy for what she had been through, or praise for having saved her father's life, Chelsea was treated like a leper for being the daughter of a criminal. In school, she was ostracized. Former friends made fun of her. She was even removed from her position in the youth group in her church. Stunned by the events that had occurred, her mother sank into deep depression. There was no one Chelsea could turn to for support or help.

The police and paramedics came in time to save her father's life, but from the moment they appeared on the scene, the grief and fear had never gone out of Chelsea's life.

Paying Pattern Penance

Chelsea began to understand that her unproductive pattern of helping others to the neglect of her own health, finances, and happiness had clear historic roots. Her father's suicide, and the events that followed, had pushed a little girl to perform acts that were far beyond the call of duty. The pattern became established. Now she always went above and beyond the call of duty with her helpfulness. And inevitably, she suffered some pain, or was unappreciated or even mistreated as a result.

As a matter of fact, she seemed to be drawn like a moth to a flame to people who would take her for granted or would use her and give nothing in return. Those were the ones who seemed to need her help most. Yet just as inevitably, they were the ones who would take advantage of her. Locked into an unproductive pattern of saving and helping others, Chelsea got grief as her reward.

When she made the connection with her past, Chelsea become quite clear in her understanding that her compulsion to keep participating in her pattern, despite its bad outcomes, was driven by a need to redeem herself and her family from community disapproval.

Shedding the Patterned Feeling

Chelsea's pattern was based on a feeling of shame and embarrassment that began with her father's suicide attempt and the humiliation that followed. She had been reacting to that and its aftermath ever since. Her pattern was motivated by the hope that one time, she would find sympathy and be rewarded for her goodness.

By gaining a *historical understanding,* Chelsea was able to connect with the feelings that drove her pattern. Upon making the historical connection, her pain and shame came pouring out. She cried and cried. For years she had felt like a bad person who had to do for others in order to redeem herself.

Now she realized that the way she always felt about herself was a direct consequence of her pattern and not a reflection on herself. This gave a great sense of relief.

She began to think of herself as a good citizen. Suddenly, Chelsea felt ready to try something she hadn't considered for years and years. Now, she could begin to set limits and looked forward to learning to say no. She was ready to stop paying penance, move to the next step of the SUBGAP method, and break the pattern that had caused her so much unhappiness.

A *historical understanding* of your pattern helps you to put the old ideas, feelings, and motivations associated with your pattern into perspective. Doing this gives you new freedom of choice. *You can choose to move on.*

CHAPTER 11

Operational Understanding

⟝⟞

WITHOUT DIGGING INTO your past very much, it is still possible to look at the motives, thoughts, and feelings that drive your patterned behavior. You can understand the specifics of how your pattern operates on a day-to-day basis, or "what makes your pattern tick." This method is called *operational understanding.*

Gaining an *operational understanding* sheds light on exactly how your unproductive pattern leads to under-achievement or underfulfillment. It is an understanding of the activity of your pattern—what your unproductive pattern does to your life to hold you back, and generally how it goes about having that impact—so you have good information to use toward breaking that pattern when you are ready.

For instance, let's look at how you understand the operation of your car. Like most of us, you may not know all the engineering principles behind the combustion engine, or how it was manufactured. But you do have a general *operational understanding* of the activity of your car. You probably know it uses a battery to get going, burns gasoline as fuel, has gears that crank the shaft that make the tires turn and brakes that make those wheels stop. And you know what to expect when you turn the key in the ignition, and step on the gas, and press the brake. You understand the operation of your car well enough to get you from place to place. You understand enough about your car to control it.

Likewise, *operational understanding* will help you to understand enough about your pattern to be able to control it.

Here and Now

An *operational understanding* of your pattern is like taking an MRI of the area of your life in which your pattern resides. Deeper than just seeing your pattern, an *operational understanding* shows you much more than you can see on the surface. It shows you the why and how of your underfulfillment *as it is occurring* in the present.

As we saw in the last chapter, sometimes even seeing your pattern does not provide sufficient energy for you to change it. This is because there are deeper components of your unproductive pattern that you need to understand first.

Developing a deeper understanding of your pattern can provide the added oomph required to break it. And it is important for you to realize that this is possible to do even *without the historical information.*

If your memories of the past are not easily unearthed, and if you are not in the frame of mind to root around in your history, developing an *operational understanding* of your pattern is the way to go. Just by understanding what makes your pattern tick in the here-and-now, an *operational understanding* will help you to tell the "me" and "not-me" of your pattern. It still helps you to free yourself from pattern-induced feelings—such as blaming yourself for missing out in your life—that bog you down. As you will see in the following example, an operational understanding helps you to understand what motivates your pattern and helps you to rise up against being controlled by it.

A Case of Operational Understanding: Holding Back the Dam

Rachel was a very strong, energetic young woman with piercing dark eyes and a competitive attitude. When she came to talk with me, she either jogged over to my office or bicycled her way there.

She was on the way to becoming a tennis champ. Her parents had been grooming her since the age of five to be able to win at Wimbledon or the Olympics. Every summer while growing up, Rachel had gone away to tennis camp, and throughout her childhood she'd always had private lessons twice a week.

The training was not wasted. Throughout her teen years, she'd steadily fought her way through the ranks of competition, finally earning a varsity tennis scholarship at a top New England college. Not only was her tuition paid, she also benefited from a foundation-fund award for talented young tennis players, which covered her expenses.

Rachel's grandfather, a former tennis coach, had played professionally when he was younger. And her older sister received a similar level of training and had already made her mark in the world of collegiate tennis. Rachel lived and breathed tennis. After graduating from college, she assisted in coaching tennis on a part-time basis while continuing to compete.

Everything in Place, Except . . .

The first time Rachel sat down in my office, it took her just a few minutes to explain her career path. It seemed like she had the chance for a promising and lively future, engaged in a sport that she truly loved.

But once her career description was finished, Rachel turned more serious. Her piercing eyes looked directly at me as she said, "I'm afraid I'm falling apart."

"What makes you feel like that?" I asked.

"It's all I've been thinking about lately. I am just so depressed these days, I just don't want to get out of bed." She paused. "What stops me from losing it completely is thinking about my mom and dad. They've been so supportive of me. They've worked so hard to get me a good life. But all I want to do is escape somewhere, so I don't have to live like this. And I don't even know why."

During the previous two or three weeks, Rachel said, she had hardly left her apartment, she'd been eating infrequently, and she had rarely picked up the phone. In fact, it was unlikely she would have made it to my office had it not been for the urging of one of her friends.

What's It All About?

These feelings weren't new, she admitted. At least a couple of times during the past year, she had suffered these similar downswings when she just didn't feel like she could go on. She wanted to hide from everyone and everything. These episodes of dark thoughts and retreat didn't seem to be connected to single events. So she didn't believe there were any particular setbacks or disappointments that could account for her feelings.

Because there was no immediately clear explanation, maybe it was "biological," one of her friends told her, and suggested that the only way out would be medication for depression—but Rachel wanted to find another way. As long as she wasn't in any danger of harming herself because of her depression, and Rachel assured me she was not, we would try the SUBGAP route first and see if the problem could also be *"pattern-o-logical."*

She seemed to become hopeful when I explained that even if a pattern could not be seen at first, there could still be one there that explained her depression, and that her problem might be resolved by using the SUBGAP method. In order for her discomfort to be quickly curtailed, Rachel and I went into emergency pattern-hunting mode in the next few sessions.

Rachel applied our top-down principle and determined that the area of her life in which there was the most glaring underfulfillment of her potential was the area of her emotions. She was deeply dissatisfied with herself and her life even though she had a lot going for her. While her life moved forward in many ways, her emotions occasionally sank into despair—for no apparent reason.

Rachel then began a bottom-up analysis of her days and nights—the nitty-gritty details of her life—to bring any hidden pattern into focus. As she described her interactions with people and recalled her behavior in the past, she began to see that one pattern kept emerging from the details. In contrast to all the negative feelings Rachel had about herself, it was striking that she never had a mean word to say about anyone. Never, ever. Nor did Rachel ever complain. Not a peep. No matter what happened to her, or what other people said to her or did that affected her, she always took the position that everything was okay.

What's Wrong with This Pattern?

What happened when Rachel's feathers were ruffled? How did she react?

Rachel realized that her pattern was to explain to herself that whatever happened was really "all for the best." Bothersome things certainly happened to her, but in her view, the best outcome would be achieved if she just didn't bother with them. She told herself, "It's unbecoming to fuss. Let these things go, and everything will eventually be fine."

For instance, Rachel described several conversations with her boyfriend during which she delicately began to state her preference or opinion about something, and her boyfriend brushed her remarks aside as silly. She said that even though it upset her for a few minutes, she was able to regain her composure and feel quiet again inside.

In examining the details of her life, Rachel certainly saw her tolerant pattern but did not necessarily think it was a bad thing. As a matter of fact, she prided herself on it. She contrasted herself positively with her sister, the "squeaky wheel," who often complained and attracted a lot of attention from her parents. And, most important, she saw absolutely no relationship between her pattern and her periodic feelings of depression. Rachel was adamant that she liked her pattern, that her pattern made her think more highly of herself, and that she had no interest in breaking it.

Understanding in the Backcourt

Then an episode occurred that introduced a little bit of *operational understanding* into Rachel's thinking about her pattern. It happened during a prestigious amateur tennis competition. The match was heated, and she was very close to making it to the playoffs, when everything was suddenly derailed by a disputed call.

As Rachel told it, she had been unfairly deprived of a point. She had made a skillful backhand shot that got by her opponent, and the line judge called it—"In!" But then the chair umpire disagreed. In the ensuing discussion, the line judge was overruled. Point, and game, went to Rachel's opponent—who ultimately won the match.

Not only did Rachel lose the match, but she saw that this judgment could significantly set back her progress through the ranks. Still, she reported that she had felt upset, sad, and angry only for a few minutes. Even when her coach and her friends urged her to contest the ruling, she refused. It was okay, she told them. She was not interested in looking like a complainer. Everything would all turn out for the best.

Her coach was beside himself. He insisted that they contest the ruling on her behalf. Rachel begged him not to do so. She didn't want to be seen as pushy or rude. Exasperated, the coach gave up.

Rachel's pattern was very much in operation during this event. She avoided unpleasantness. She wanted to be "nice" no matter what the circumstance. She didn't want to upset anyone. She didn't want to cause trouble for the judge, or her opponent. Unwilling to complain, Rachel had an image of herself as easygoing and at peace with herself. But, this time, as much as she tried to put the match behind her, the memory of her missed chance stuck with her, it didn't go away in a few days and, instead, she fell into another one of her depressions.

For the first time in her life, her pattern didn't seem so harmless. She realized upon reflection that her self-image of an unflappable and accepting person was in conflict with the reality of the situation. For if she were truly peaceable and easy-going, why did she have these periods of depressive and hopeless thinking, when all she wanted to do was disappear?

Rachel suddenly had a glimpse of *operational understanding*. She exclaimed, "I'm just like Hans Brinker in the story *Hans Brinker and the Silver Skates*!"

When I inquired as to how she saw herself as similar, she

explained. In the story, Hans was willing to miss out on winning the silver skates in the skating competition because, on the way to the competition, he saw some holes in the dike. The whole town was in danger. Forfeiting the competition, he plugged up the holes with his fingers and stayed there to hold back the floodwaters.

Instead of letting her feelings out, Rachel was holding her emotions in for fear of a flood that would bother others. She said, "I tell myself that I do my pattern to keep everyone else comfortable, I think I'm doing it to save *them* and it never occurred to me that it hurts *me*."

Although she had seen her pattern, she never before understood how it impacted her life. Now she saw that her negative emotional energy didn't just go away when fleeting feelings of disappointment faded. Instead, those feelings were being stored up somewhere in her system, somewhere in her unconscious.

Rachel understood that frequent small episodes of negative emotions built to a critical mass. Sooner or later, all those dammed-up emotions broke through, like water bursting through the dike, causing her depressed feelings that stayed with her until they ran their course and then the pattern would start again. This was indeed a good *operational understanding of* how her pattern functioned in her daily life.

Match Point

Rachel didn't need to understand her history or how the pattern originated to understand why and how the pattern deprived her of both achievement and emotional stability.

Finally, she was ready to break her pattern and to find out what she could do to prevent the emotions from "backing up" in this way. Instead of dismissing her negative emotions, when they occurred, instead of putting her fingers in the dike and holding everything back, she needed to let the feelings surface in her mind, recognize them, respect them, and take appropriate action to make a more positive outcome possible. She was encouraged about the possibilities if she broke her pattern—if she allowed herself to feel her feelings and then started *acting* on her own behalf.

Rachel was ready to move on to the next step of the SUBGAP method, and she did it by understanding her pattern in the here-and-now.

Operational understanding may not bring with it the added depth of historical understanding—but don't underestimate its power. Either form of understanding gives you enough of a handle on your pattern to get the job done. That job is the one that lies ahead in the next step of the SUBGAP method—*breaking* your pattern.

PART FOUR

Breaking

～

Decisions determine destiny.

—Frederick Speakman

CHAPTER 12

How to Break Your Patterns

~

NOW THAT YOU have learned the methods for *seeing* and *understanding* your pattern, are you ready to learn how to *break* it? Are you ready to change your life?

It's time to cut to the heart of the matter.

Once you have learned to *see* and *understand* your pattern, you will become aware of your pattern at the moment when it tries to control you. It is inevitable that you will come face to face with your pattern with great regularity because, as we have discussed, your pattern is intertwined with your daily life. That means that after having mastered the first two steps of the SUBGAP method, you are in a position to *break* your pattern every time it occurs. That could be once a week, once a day, or even several times a day. The point is: there are many opportunities.

Now that you can notice your pattern, what do you do to break it when you see it coming? Let's take it step by step.

It's a Process!

Changing long-standing lifestyle behaviors is not going to occur overnight. It needs to be approached bit by bit. Please keep in mind that pattern breaking is, after all, a process. It is a new skill that you will pick up gradually over time. And like any other skill, pattern-breaking improves with practice.

Some people are good at adopting the attitude of a beginner; others are not. If you are someone who can cut yourself some slack while you're starting to practice the skill of pattern breaking, maybe you can begin to do it right away without a lot of stress.

Sure, you'll feel like kicking yourself now and then, when you slip into the old pattern and let it control your actions or reactions. Those opportunities are the ones that get away. But don't worry, there will be others. Likewise, you will feel proud of yourself and exhilarated each time you succeed in heading off your pattern at the pass. And I should tell you that you have a really wonderful surprise waiting for you the first time you break your pattern. Like the people in the upcoming chapters, you will be really delighted at your sense of mastery the first time you get all the way through step 3 of the

SUBGAP method. The first time you *see, understand,* and actually *break* your pattern, it is really a thrill.

Can you remember a time when you mastered something that seemed daunting or out of reach? Do you recall the first time you rode a bicycle without training wheels; or made it down a ski slope without falling; or hit a home run? Mastery is exhilarating. Once you've tasted the success of breaking your pattern, even if it is in a small way, you will be very motivated to do it again and again. You will feel that you are the boss of your own life, instead of being subject to following your unproductive pattern's blueprint. The thrill of being free from your pattern's control will be memorable, and the result of living more in tune with fulfilling your potential will be something you will want to repeat. The key to the *breaking* process is breaking your pattern *once*—everything else will follow from that.

But, try not to be too demanding on yourself. You can't expect to get an "A" in pattern breaking right away. No one can. If you have a tendency to be performance-driven, I'd urge you to take it a bit easy on yourself as you go through this process. Even if you tend to learn other things fast, this process is an exception. It takes time to learn to break your pattern on a consistent basis.

Just think about how long your pattern has been sitting there in your unconscious mind, mostly hidden just under the surface like that giant iceberg we discussed at the beginning of this book. Your unproductive pattern may have been entrenching itself inside your mind for years, and in some cases, decades. That doesn't mean that it can't be broken, it just means you have to go easy on yourself in terms of your pace, when it comes to applying the SUBGAP method.

You Can Beat Your Pattern

Your pattern is not so tough as it may seem. Sure, it has been making you participate in behaviors that are not so productive. Certainly it has held you back from fulfilling your potential in one or more areas of your life. But it only was able to do so because it operated in secret.

Your pattern is not unbreakable and its hold on you, although it may have lasted a long time, is not as tight as you might think. Your pattern has been all smoke and mirrors, and it has led you to think, feel, and act in ways that were not in your best interest. Like the Wizard of Oz, the wizard looks so threatening, powerful, and bigger than life but it is actually quite mortal and not such a challenging opponent once you see and understand the little man behind the screen. But now that you can see and understand how your pattern has been leading you on a detour from your true goals, you can overthrow your pattern. It's not so tough.

I will tell you flat out and without hesitation, *no pattern is unbreakable!*

Though first successes may be small, they are consummately rewarding. It's a great feeling when you realize you've actually stopped your pattern for the first time. Right there, you start to realize that you can slowly but surely gain control over you life. And that is invigorating!

Now, Let's Get Busy!

There are many ways to *break* a pattern. Everyone's pattern is different. However, the overall method is the same no matter what the circumstances. Use the SUBGAP methods of *seeing* and *understanding* to get to that spot where the two paths through your life are clear, then use a pattern-breaking technique to make the right choice.

In the next chapters we'll look at three of the most effective methods that I've taught in my office for many years, and which have helped many people make that first big break and achieve dominance over their patterns. They are:

1. *The Rapid Correction Method.*
2. *The Tao of Pattern Breaking Method.*
3. *Breaking by Letting Go.*

As the case examples in the next three chapters illustrate, there is sometimes a moment in the unfolding of a pattern that gives you a chance to break free and improve the outcome of situation. That moment reveals the "weak spot" in your pattern.

Your pattern's weak spots are places in you life where the road forks—where you can choose to take the patterned path, or to break with that path and choose a better direction. *Making the right choice at these points gives you a wonderful opportunity to halt your pattern.*

CHAPTER 13

The Rapid Correction Method

THE GREAT WRITER and humanitarian Pearl Buck once wrote, "Every great mistake has a halfway moment, a split-second when it can be . . . remedied." The same is true of your unproductive patterns. As you are tempted to participate in your pattern's typical steps, and right before you are led completely astray, there is a moment when you are teetering on the edge of that pattern. Before you've jumped into unproductive behavior there is still time to catch yourself, regain your balance, and make a better choice. That teetering-on-the-edge moment, that potential misstep on the high wire of life, is where the *rapid correction* method comes in to break your pattern.

When you have taken the first two steps in the SUBGAP method—you can see your pattern and have a way to understand it—you will probably find that you can become intensely aware of the characteristic signs of that pattern. For instance, Alexa, the woman I'm about to describe, reported that before applying the SUBGAP method, she didn't even notice her pattern, but after learning to *see* and *understand* her pattern, its warning signs were as ominous as "hearing the theme music from *Jaws*."

Whatever the warning sign, it signals that you're headed into trouble, precisely because you're about to follow a pattern that leaves you unfulfilled. That's when you have the opportunity to apply the *rapid correction* method.

Rapid correction involves the same mechanism that we all use when we are changing lanes on the expressway. Your unproductive pattern is riding alongside of you, but out of sight in your blind spot and ready to cause a crash. As you're moving ahead, about to change lanes to pass, you glance over your shoulder and—there it is, your pattern, veering into your lane. In that moment, you need to swerve to avoid a collision. If you react quickly enough, you can avoid certain damage.

Rapid correction is different than already falling into the pattern and then having to pull yourself out. Instead it is like getting a glimpse of a problem before it happens, and then veering back to the right path before any pattern-related damage can be done.

A Memorable Performance: A Case of Rapid Correction

Alexa is a talented stage actress who studied acting at one of the most famous acting studios in the world. By the time she came to talk with me, she had performed with some of the most famous screen and stage actors of our time. Her performances were noticed and received accolades from reviewers who, again and again, singled her out for praise.

For a woman with all of this talent and potential, one would think that her career would have skyrocketed her to success. But, instead, there had been very little momentum in her career. Her opportunity to perform was infrequent. And this was what she came to me to talk about.

The reality was, Alexa found herself with a lot of downtime between roles. She was very disappointed that none of the directors or producers from previous productions kept in touch with her, took her calls, or answered her letters, and that they never considered casting her in new productions even if her performance with them had received praise.

Clearly this was an instance of unfulfilled career potential. A top-down hunt wasn't even required. What was wrong with the picture of Alexa's life was glaring, and it just didn't make sense to her

When Alexa began to discuss the problem with me, it all seemed very mysterious. No particular pattern seemed apparent (but when it comes to patterns, this is often the case at first glance). It was clear that by nature Alexa was a good-hearted person. She was also attractive, stylish, and customarily polite to colleagues and directors.

Nor did the problem lie in her acting—certainly not that. She learned her roles quickly and well and brought depth and nuance to even small roles. She was never late to rehearsals and never missed a cue or botched the staging. It had to be that an unproductive pattern was hidden some-where in her professional life that led to her underachieve-ment in the acting world.

Furthermore, if there was a pattern, then that pattern must have been adversely affecting the motivation of directors and theater companies when it came to casting her again. In other words, even though Alexa's pattern wasn't clear, we had ample evidence of its presence. Something was affecting the impres-sion that she made on directors. Whatever that "something" was, its impact must have been negative.

All the World's a Stage . . . for Patterns

Indeed, while conducting a bottom-up analysis by reviewing the nitty-gritty details of her participation in the last few pro-ductions, Alexa found a number of interesting occurrences. In one instance, while rehearsing for a lead role in an Off-Broadway production, she reported that she missed two rehearsals out of about twenty. Her reason, at the time, had seemed more than justified. One of her lifelong friends was getting married on a Saturday afternoon in upstate New York.

Following the theater company's required protocol for such situations, Alexa contacted the director and requested the two days off that she would need. The director stated that she preferred that Alexa not miss the rehearsals. But, at the same time, the director said she understood that this was Alexa's good friend and was important to her. Alexa got permission to go, and missed a Saturday and a Sunday rehearsal. Her friend, naturally, was very appreciative to have Alexa at the wedding.

When Alexa returned, rehearsals went well and the show opened with a very positive audience reaction. She received many compliments from the director and the show's opening was followed by great reviews, especially for her perform-ance. So far, so good, and so far it was the same as Alexa had experienced time and time again. Good work, great reviews, and then *dropped like a hot potato.*

In the months following that success, the director mounted several more productions. Other cast members from the original production were given new parts. But the director had never contacted Alexa.

One episode of this kind did not suggest a pattern. But as Alexa continued to review the details of her professional life, another instance stood out.

She'd had a supporting role in a London production of a popular play. After one of the performances, her agent called her and told her that he had invited one of the assistant artistic directors of a major Shakespeare festival in England to see her performance. That assistant director did indeed see the show and was so impressed that he asked Alexa to read for a part in an upcoming Shakespearean production that he was mounting the next season.

However, as Alexa's luck would have it, auditions were going to be held at the same time as one of her matinee performances of the play in London. Since her role was only a supportive one, and she had an understudy to take over if necessary, she asked the assistant director for permission to attend the audition. The assistant director told her it would be no problem, but phoned later that evening to say that her director wanted her to *explain* why she was going to miss the matinee production.

Alexa met with the director, explained the opportunity, and immediately the atmosphere in the office got rather chilly. Without a moment's hesitation, the director said, "No."

Shocked by his response, Alexa was speechless. She began to cry. The director said he was sorry, but that was his decision. During the rest of the production, he remained cool toward her.

Once again, as usual, she received very positive notices in the London papers—remarkable, given the fact that she had only played a supporting role. Yet, sure enough, when the director and producers began casting subsequent productions, Alexa was overlooked while others in the cast were not.

A Pattern of Expecting Help

In those two instances there were too many parallels to ignore. Both times, Alexa had perfectly good reasons to request time off, and in both cases she followed protocol. But there was no doubting that, in both situations, she had done something that curried disfavor with her directors. Clearly, a pattern of asking for permission to be excused was related to, if not the cause of, not being considered in future casting.

Was something particularly mean-spirited about the directors? Or could it be that there something particularly off-putting about the manner in which Alexa approached them? In trying to understand this pattern in depth, Alexa began to use a historical approach and, in reviewing her student days, exactly the opposite picture came into focus.

Throughout high school, college, and then at the acting studio, she was the darling of her teachers. Alexa reported that she had attended a performing arts high school and got a lot of support from the teachers who helped her gain admission to a college with a great acting program, after which she attended an acting studio in New York City where she was the star of master classes with famous actors. She felt tremendously supported and helped by her teachers and school administrators, and blossomed in those environments.

Even before that, her mother did everything possible to make Alexa's dream of becoming an actress come true, and saved her pennies to pay for the acting lessons. When teenage Alexa got roles in summer stock companies, her mother even rented a little apartment near the beach, and spent summers with her near the theater company so her daughter would have an easy time taking advantage of an opportunity to perform there.

A historical approach made Alexa aware that her supportive experiences caused her to take for granted that people in the real acting world would be as helpful and encouraging as people had been in her school career. Of course, this didn't turn out to be the case.

Alexa began to understand that she approached every director and theater company administrator with the assumption that they would, of course, want to help and take good care of her. Instead, the reality was that in the real acting world, the success of the production was paramount to those in charge. Alexa didn't take this into account. It wasn't all completely clear yet, but she was starting to see and understand her pattern.

Before she had a chance to arrive at a complete understanding her pattern, Alexa's investigation had to be put on hold and she postponed further talks with me, because another job arrived. She was offered a terrific opportunity—an understudy position in a production of a Chekhov play. The main cast was adorned with a host of famous names, and the odds were in her favor that at some point in the production Alexa would have the opportunity to fill in for one of the leads and a star could be born!

To Pattern or Not to Pattern, That Is the Question

For several weeks, I didn't hear from Alexa. Nor did I expect to, since I knew that her rehearsals were all-consuming. Then I received an urgent phone call. Alexa spoke quietly, saying she was calling from her cell phone. She was standing outside of the stage entrance, rehearsals were still going on, but there was something she *had* to tell me.

With all the excitement of the Chekhov play, Alexa reported, she had forgotten about a commitment she had made to a local theater company in her hometown in New Jersey. She had promised the local group that she would perform the lead role in a one-time performance of a musical comedy. Her whole family—even aunts and uncles—had all bought tickets to see her and planned a party for her afterward. How could she let them down?

Just one night off—that was all she needed. Alexa had

performed the intended musical comedy role many times before. She could sneak in the little amount of rehearsal time she needed without missing any Chekhov run-throughs. As luck would have it, the musical comedy overlapped with only one rehearsal of the Chekhov play. Since she was "only an understudy," she had decided that it was perfectly reasonable to ask for a one-night leave.

Alexa told me that she had just come from talking to the director's assistant and then phoned me. In her hand was an "Excused Leave of Absence" form. She had filled it out properly and was about to turn it in.

But then—and this was where Alexa described the "funny feeling" she got—as she had begun to fill out the form to submit to the director's assistant, she said she could almost literally hear a deep, thrumming warning music in her head—warning of impending danger—similar to the ominous theme right before the shark attack in *Jaws*.

The leave of absence form was still in her hand. But instead of turning it in, she had made the call to me.

A Rapid Correction

While filling out the form, Alexa suddenly understood that the director wasn't her mother, the director wasn't her drama teacher at the high school of performing arts, the director wasn't a teacher in a master class, the director *was* trying to make the best production of this Chekhov play. She understood the director's point of view and decided to respect it.

"Listen to this!" announced Alexa. And the next thing I heard was the sound of tearing paper. "I tore it up, and I broke my pattern. Just wanted to let you know!"

I congratulated her. Alexa reported feeling a strong wave of relief. More than that, she felt proud of herself. Not only had she sensed the warning signs of her pattern arising, but she had also managed to take an action, do a *rapid correction,* and called me as her witness.

Several weeks later, I heard from her again. Alexa reported that the director had asked her to read for a part in an upcoming production. This reinforcement, and reward, came with such immediacy that Alexa felt she had all the proof she needed that she had broken the curse of her pattern.

With *rapid correction,* she had broken her unproductive pattern. True, it had just happened once—but the evidence that even that first *breaking* event made a difference was right in front of her. It was a very positive indicator that if she continued breaking her unproductive pattern, she could indeed fulfill her potential and quite possibly be on the road to stardom.

You, too, can turn the tide at the critical moment and begin to see your potential fulfilled. Instead of losing control and letting your pattern take over, you can use *rapid correction* so that what might otherwise have been a setback becomes merely a "close call." *What a relief!*

CHAPTER 14

The Tao of Pattern Breaking

⁓

THE FIRST METHOD of pattern breaking involved taking a quick action. The second method of breaking a pattern requires inaction. Instead of quickly shifting from a patterned direction to an unpatterned one—as in the *rapid correction* method—the *tao of pattern breaking* method employs intentional inactivity. By using this method, you hit the pause button long enough for your pattern to miss its chance to take control of a situation in your life. You simply resist the impulse to act, and take a wait-and-see attitude instead. This is a good method to use if your emotions tend to launch you into your patterned actions so fast that you don't notice until it is too late.

If you can pause rather than proceed in your patterned way, and "let the chips fall where they may," the situation might unfold differently just because you don't insert your usual patterned behavior into it. Then, you might just find yourself being "more in the flow" of life (as the Taoist masters would say) and less in your pattern. Something new and better might happen naturally.

Putting all action on hold when you find yourself in that precarious moment in which you are in danger of participating in your pattern, might just keep the pattern from inserting itself at a critical juncture. Once that critical juncture has passed, the impulse to take patterned action may also pass. Then it will be too late for the pattern to do its damage.

I realize that may sound a little bit abstract. I promise it will all become crystal clear when I discuss the story of "John the Doer" later in this chapter. But before I describe John, it's important to say a few words about the philosophy behind this approach. For many of us who have a "can-do attitude," the whole notion of "doing nothing" to deal with a situation may seem strange and exotic.

Learn the "Way of Breaking"

Taoism is based on the idea that there is a naturally positive flow to all things in the universe. It is pretty safe to assume that your unproductive pattern is the unnatural course of events, and a more naturally positive path for your life has to be found.

The inspiration for this method of pattern breaking comes from my years of study as the first Western student of Dr. D. S. Rhee, a Buddhist-Taoist psychotherapy master renowned throughout Asia. One of the things I learned is that most people in the world these days—whether in the East or the West—have an *action* mindset. That is, we have generally accepted the notion, and subscribed to the belief, that problems can only be solved through activity.

I discovered, however, that the unique way of looking at the world from a Buddhist-Taoist perspective can offer the possibility of solving problems in a way that just isn't available to the "can-do" mentality. When a pattern impels you toward a *wrong action* and you can't come up with the right action, your best defense—indeed, your rescue—can be accomplished through *inactivity.*

Doing nothing is most difficult when you feel an almost overwhelming need to *do something.* Just consider the way most of us react when our emotions are telling us that we urgently need to take some action. It's like having a voice in your head that keeps repeating, insistently, "You cannot leave the situation as it is!" Of course, the action we launch into at that moment might be the first step in an unproductive pattern.

When your pattern is stimulated by your emotions, it is extra hard to take a step back and think productively. But sometimes, that's exactly what's called for. There are some situations in which you simply need to slow down events to control them. Some patterns go from zero to sixty in five seconds flat. If you don't find a way to slow them down, they play out automatically with lightning speed, and your life is not under your control.

Tao of Pattern Breaking: Story of John the Doer

John, a high-school science teacher in his early thirties, is the very definition of action. Everything he does, he does 200 percent!

Teaching in a small town in Maine, he has taken on many roles. He is the school's baseball coach, advisor for the after-school science club, and a Sunday-school teacher at his church. He is married (his wife is also a teacher) and has two young sons, who provide another opportunity for John to keep moving and stay involved. He assists the coaches on his sons' soccer team, is the travel team coach when the team plays in a neighboring town, and has never missed a game.

When I first met John, I got an immediate impression of someone with a military background. Sure enough, he told me he was had served in Desert Storm, and received a bronze star for bravery. He still says, "Yes, sir!" to anyone older than him, and has the most "can-do" attitude of anyone in his town.

John doesn't touch alcohol because, as an adult child of an

alcoholic, he vowed never to walk in the footsteps of his own, abrasively loud-mouthed, father's footsteps. His father was, as John described him, a "very nasty drunk."

But despite his success in staying away from alcohol, some of his father's behavior has begun to creep into John's. He tells me there are moments when all of his good efforts go "out the window."

At these times, he exhibits what he calls "dry drunk" behavior. He turns nasty and mean, treating his own wife and kids just as his own father used to treat John's mother, John, and his brothers. He admitted that this was an extremely unproductive pattern in his life and one he really wanted to change.

Good Intentions and Bad Patterns

John was very honest in describing these outbursts in which, in his own opinion, he had taken on his father's pattern. He told me he would find himself yelling, grabbing one of the kids by the shoulders, yelling some more, and concocting punishments. Whenever his boys acted up, he felt as if a switch was flipped, the pattern would go into full gear, and he just had to do something immediately to correct their behavior.

Even in public, John could lose control. He developed a very bad reputation on the soccer field for yelling at his sons when they didn't live up to his behavior standards. In the face of repeated public humiliation, his boys began to show less and less self-control on the field. They began to get into fights in the middle of games and started clowning around so badly that the coach sometimes had to pull them from the field.

It was obvious to John that this pattern had led to a very bad cycle developing between he and his sons. But despite his seeing the pattern, and despite his historical understanding, without a method to apply he couldn't stop himself. John could never tell when he was going to burst into a rage. Again and again, things would happen that made him lose his temper.

The Son and the Moon

Things came to a head the day John blew up in front of everyone in his neighborhood. It occurred on a Saturday afternoon.

John's house was at the end of a cul de sac on a suburban road. A number of houses had windows that looked out on a field where the kids liked to play.

As John was passing his living room window that morning, he noticed his younger son, Benjy, out on the playing field. In recent months, Benjy had turned more and more antic. He was widely regarded as "the class clown." True to form, Benjy was acting up. As John glanced out the window, he saw his son drop his pants and "moon" another kid.

In an instant the patterned switch was flipped and John was out of the house, bellowing his son's name, "Benjy!" "Ben-jy!!" "Be-n-n-jy-y!!!!!"

As John tore across the field, neighbors came running out to look. They saw a man out of control. He crossed the field like a runaway freight train, bellowing wildly, grabbed his son by the arm, and dragged him back into the house.

When John's wife tried to intervene, he turned his wrath on her. Benjy needed to be grounded, he insisted—and not just for a day, but for a long, long time. As his wife started to protest, he lambasted her for being too soft. Now in tears, she was terror-stricken by her husband's behavior. She fled, grabbing the children, and drove to her mother's house.

That was the line in the sand for John. This couldn't go on. He told me he was willing to *do anything* to break his pattern.

Here was a heroic man, someone who had risked his life to save his buddies in the Gulf War. In a heartbeat, he would have laid down his life to help his wife or kids. Yet he couldn't stop himself from being verbally abusive to them. He could see his pattern, he had a historical understanding, now he was ready for a strong method to break the pattern.

I summarized it to him this way: "John, I know you are a good man. I know you would throw yourself in front of a speeding train if it was necessary to save your family. But for some reason, you can't protect them from your own temper. What do you make of that?"

This tough guy's eyes welled up. "I know!" he said. "Every time I get ticked off I lose control."

"What makes you lose control?"

He thought for a minute before he answered. "It's all my responsibility. When my kids do the wrong thing, it's *up to me* to do something about it. I feel like I have to do something right away. Then, the next thing I know, I'm yelling at them and pushing them around. I know it's not the right thing to do."

"What would happen," I wondered aloud, "if you just did nothing?"

"Nothing?" He gave me a quizzical look.

"That's right. Just do *nothing* long enough until you figure out the right thing to do. Sometimes, if you take this pause, you break the momentum of the pattern instead of feeding into it. Do you think you can do it?"

I was describing the *tao of pattern breaking* method and John, who loved his kids and hated that he often acted like he didn't, sincerely wanted to try it.

Here Goes Nothing!

The next time John talked to me, he reported an incident in

which he'd had the opportunity to give the *tao of pattern breaking* method a trial run.

Arriving home from work one night, he stepped inside and planted his foot squarely into a puddle of milk and cereal. A rush of emotion came over him. He felt like yelling something. How had his wife let this happen? His boys were out of control again! It was up to him to do something about it.

In an instant, he opened his mouth to bellow out the rage that was ready to make him burst. Then he caught sight of the boys hovering nearby, just bracing themselves for their father to explode. John opened his mouth. The words started coming out sharp and hard. "What—is—going—on—here?!"

And at that moment John remembered the *tao of pattern breaking*. He knew that the pattern of yelling was about to begin. John was like a man trying to keep a hurricane from blowing open his front door. It took every ounce of his energy. But he held himself back.

It was a tough moment. The pressure to take some sort of action was tremendous. The pressure to participate in the pattern was overwhelming. But the berating words that were right on the tip of his tongue never came out of his mouth. He stood his ground against the emotion of the pattern. He *did nothing* for a few seconds.

Suddenly, out of the storm inside of himself, he calmly saw something very surprising. He saw that both boys had paper towels in their hands.

He saw that his six-year-old was crouching down and had started to mop up the mess. He saw that his older son, the ten-year-old, was about to join his brother in the clean-up. Doing nothing allowed John to notice things about the situation he had never noticed before. Doing nothing prevented the pattern from taking over at the moment it usually did. Instead, he saw that his boys were trying to handle the situation, together, and make it right. And John's storm went away as rapidly as it arrived.

"Good job, boys," he said.

John took off his coat, walked into his living room, turned on the TV, and sat down on the couch while his sons finished mopping up the spill.

For the first time, John had broken the pattern that endangered the happiness of his family. This "doer" was amazed that he solved the problem by doing nothing. John will have to practice this many more times for it to become easier to consistently break his pattern, but he has made the leap into the breaking stage of the SUBGAP method with that first success.

Wait Your Way to Success

It takes a lot of effort to control yourself and do nothing when every bone in your body is telling you that you have to do something, meaning *do* your pattern, or you'll simply explode.

But you are *not* going to explode. As a matter of fact, if you do nothing just long enough for your pattern to miss its chance to take over, you may instead find the naturally right answer.

At first, you may find that it's so difficult to stay uninvolved in what's going on that you have to physically leave the situation. If the pull to do your pattern is so strong, and you can't control your feelings enough to do nothing, then leave. Try to get your feelings under control, doing nothing, in a nearby, quiet location. Take a time-out. Go to another room or step outside.

If you have a pattern that accelerates rapidly, the only way to break it is to slow everything down. With a lightning-speed pattern that is driven by strong feelings, anything you do at the moment your pattern hits might feed into it. But, if you decide to simply stand still, your pattern's moment to control you might just pass right by you.

If you use the *tao of pattern breaking* method—and break your pattern by "not-doing"—you may be pleasantly surprised to find yourself getting into the flow of your life without the hindrance of unproductive patterns.

CHAPTER 15

Breaking by Letting Go

THERE'S A FUNNY thing about us human beings, and that is the far-reaching nature of our sense of nostalgia. We have nostalgic feelings about just about any part of our history. We even have a special feeling about the unpleasant parts of our past. We can be nostalgic for almost anything we ever owned, even if it is an old suit of clothes that is out of style or doesn't fit, or a raggedy old teddy bear. If it represents some part of our history, we want to hold onto it.

The same is true about our patterns. There are aspects to our patterns, even if unproductive, that we might miss if we gave them up. Even if we realize we have outgrown them and that it is time to move on, they still possess some appeal.

Patterns sometimes provide certain comforts. They can keep us in a familiar safety zone that is soothing in a way, even while holding us back from achievement and fulfillment. If your pattern provides you with some of these "perks," there is a good chance that, when breaking your pattern, you will also miss a certain sense of security it gave you.

The third way of breaking your patterns is *breaking by letting go* of those comforts that tie you to your pattern. In this technique you familiarize yourself with the comforts you gain from participating in your pattern, repeatedly weigh them against what your pattern costs you in terms of fulfillment, and—only when you are really ready—intentionally decide to give up your pattern's perks.

When your pattern provides you with a perk that comforts you in some way, giving up that solace for the greater reward of fulfilling your potential can break that pattern's grip on your life. It is an easy choice once you realize what is at stake, but not such an easy thing to actually do.

As you'll see in the following example, this form of pattern breaking takes a little time, since you have to think about and *weigh your life choices,* and come to a decision that you are ready to let go of the perks the pattern offers to gain a better life. You might have to come to that choice point more than a few times before you finally make the leap of saying, "I pass" on this round of your pattern. Everything I've witnessed and experienced convinces me that the price you pay for breaking unproductive patterns, and pushing yourself past those old comfort zones is absolutely worth the gain.

If I ever want to remind myself of that, I simply think of the case of Jenny Lee and her mother, Michele. Their story illustrates the miraculous changes that affect our lives for the better when old patterns are finally broken and left behind, even if old comforts have to be relinquished in the *breaking by letting go* process.

A Case of Breaking by Letting Go: The Pattern's Perk

Michele was a woman who obviously gained a great deal of comfort from being told what to do. Whenever she became confused or uncertain about what was best for herself, she would consult with her mother, her sister, her best friend from college, or her lunchtime colleague—anyone but herself.

Beyond that, she would look at her horoscope, read Ann Landers and Dear Abby, consult a "psychic," or get a tarot card reading. The whole, elaborate decision-making process occurred whether she had to make an important choice, such as whether to relocate to another city for a new job—or something as relatively minor, such as which movie to rent over the weekend. Eventually, armed with all these opinions, she would make a decision based on majority opinion and proceed with her life.

Not surprisingly, Michele never felt that her life was her own or that she could really do what she wanted to. Worse yet, if thrown back on her own resources, without any outside opinions at all, she felt completely unable to figure out what *she* wanted to do in any of these situations. She had become so reliant on outside opinions that she almost lived her life on the basis of what other people thought was best for her. She felt that this had a margin of safety for her and she didn't have to be afraid that she was making a wrong choice if lots of other people agreed about what she should do.

She was living *as if* she were Michele, but she was actually living the life that the majority opinion of a committee of decision makers deemed proper for her. She had a very small role in choosing her own destiny. Of course, it is impossible to be fulfilled when operating this way. Michele was able to *see* her pattern, but was too timid and afraid that her sense of security would be lost if she gave it up.

This sense of security is the perk that tied Michele to her pattern.

Needless to say, all the people who gave her advice could not possibly know how to choose as correct and fulfilling a path as she could. No committee could have the deep inner sense of direction that existed buried somewhere within Michele's mind and heart. In fact, the committee never took account of Michele's own opinions. And Michele herself was out of touch with most of her own opinions.

Pattern's Cost: What She Wanted Most

Despite the safety and comfort that her committee seemed to provide, Michele had sufficient self-awareness to feel that something was acutely missing in her life. She had felt a growing desire to have a child. Michele deeply and truly wanted to be a mommy.

From the moment she allowed herself to think seriously about this possibility, Michele braced herself to deal with all the reasons why such a step was impossible. Foremost among her worries was that, unmarried and with no steady partner, she would have to face being a single mother.

Of course, following her usual pattern, Michele consulted with her committee. Though opinions varied, Michele's consultants generally agreed that she couldn't handle adopting a child, that this step would be wrong for her. Afraid of further discouragement from her committee, Michele came to talk with me about her wish.

For once, her committee's advice didn't sit well with her. She had tried to maintain her placid attitude—tried to convince herself that motherhood was just "not meant to be"—but all the while, she was disturbed by the discrepancy between her own real need and the cautions of relatives, friends, tarot card readings, and advice columnists.

Michele's mother was the most adamant. She discouraged her daughter from adopting because she felt that Michele was too frail a person to handle being a single parent. Besides, her mother asked pointedly, "Wouldn't you be embarrassed in church on Sundays—bringing a child without a husband?"

Michele's father felt that she would never be able to support herself and a child on her librarian's income. From her lunchtime friend at work, she heard that the best policy was to wait and redouble her efforts to find a husband first.

And then there were the signs and signals that she followed. The fortune teller told Michele she would find a good husband soon and she wouldn't have to wait too long to fulfill her dream in a manner that everyone would approve. Her horoscopes kept saying things like, "Try to wait until all the dust settles before making any decisions," "You know you're waiting for something, but you also know your patience will pay off."

For the first time in years, Michele discovered that she was taking no comfort from handing over her decision-making responsibilities. Her restlessness grew ever more visible as her forty-seventh birthday approached. Finally, Michele *decided* that something had to be done.

From her research, Michele had learned that the adoption of very young children was usually restricted to younger mothers. As she envisioned her future relationship with an adopted child, she wanted to play a role in the child's early development. So the pressure was on. If she really wanted a young child, she couldn't delay much longer. That is when she came to talk with me about it.

Understanding the Fear of Letting Go

In reviewing the details of her life, Michele started to see her pattern clearly. Still, the prospect of going against the tide, making her own decision against the advice of her "committee" made her very, very nervous. She didn't want to give up the sense of relief she obtained from giving away responsibility for her life and she didn't want to feel the anxiety over deciding her own destiny, since she was such a fearful person.

What if her relatives, friends, co-workers were all right and she was wrong? What if she were biting off more than she could chew with this adoption?

Michele discovered that there were many reasons for her pattern of reliance on others. Using a historical approach to understand her pattern, it became clear to Michele that both of her parents had been overprotective throughout her childhood. She almost never went anywhere or did anything by herself because her parents were so concerned that "nothing bad ever happen to her."

In talking about her pattern, Michele came to understand that it was based on a fear that she would be in danger if she ever did something independently. Even in early adulthood, her attempts at independence had been foiled by all the warnings of danger.

Using an operational approach to understanding her pattern threw more light on Michele's situation. It was clear that whenever she wanted to avoid bouts of overwhelming anxiety, she could fall back on her pattern and let others run her life. Her familiar reliance on others was her pattern's security blanket, it made her feel "safe."

But how safe was it really, if the thing she wanted most would be sacrificed in the name of that safety? When she understood exactly what her pattern was costing her, her perspective changed.

Leaping to China

By seeing her pattern and understanding what was at stake, Michele knew that she could no longer tolerate delegating the decision of adoption to her committee—especially if she was ever to feel fulfilled in this important way.

As I said previously, there are many ways to break a pattern, and Michele accomplished this by using the *breaking by letting go* process of constantly comparing the patterned path with the independent one that held a chance for her dream to be fulfilled. Michele prepared herself to break her pattern by a process of eroding the pattern's grip upon her over time. She compared and contrasted, day in and day out, until the choice was clear—frightening, but clear.

Without a doubt, she would be forced to lose the solace that her pattern provided if she wanted to gain what she really wanted deep down. Michele went through the process of *weighing* the differences between her patterned and unpatterned paths daily. After a few months of comparing her choices, and looking at her life with and without breaking her pattern, she *intentionally chose to leave her comfort zone.*

Ultimately, she proceeded with the paperwork, the interviews, and home visits. After several months she was accepted as a prospective adoptive parent by a Chinese orphanage. Michele's willingness to take on the challenge meant that she was willing to *let go* of the comforts of her pattern and was ready to make that trade-off.

Word came that her child was ready. Michele received a report and a picture of her new toddler-age daughter, along with the date by which she would need to be at the orphanage in Jiang Xi province. Michele was not only ready to do it, but also insistent enough to persuade her sister to come along.

In due course, Michele and her sister left with paperwork, passports, stuffed animals, and phrasebooks in hand. They returned, exhausted and frazzled, with many interesting stories to tell, and with one very beautiful and spirited toddler named Jiang Li, which means "beautiful river" in Chinese. Michele thought that this sounded like Jenny Lee and started using the Chinese and this adoptive name interchangeably when speaking to her new daughter.

As soon as she arrived back in the States, her anxiety and doubts about her own competence set in. "What have I done?" she kept asking herself. "Am I going to ruin my life and my daughter's life, too?"

Assailed by concerns about her inability to care for herself and Jenny, Michele started to wonder whether Jenny would have been better off staying in the orphanage. Or perhaps the child would be better off with a more secure and competent adoptive parent than herself.

Darkest before the Dawn

In the weeks after Jenny came to live with her, Michele frequently phoned her mother to ask for advice or help. Her mother responded with a lot of, "I told you so" remarks, which only intensified Michele's panic.

Indeed, for the first months after returning home it seemed that her two worst fears had come true. It felt overwhelming to her to negotiate life with a toddler by herself, and it seemed that her mother was ignoring her and avoiding contact with her.

As the pressure mounted, Michele took a family leave from work. Before long, she returned to the office, but now she had an added concern—that her inability to put in the long research hours (as she had in the past) would cause her to lose her job.

And then there was Jenny to worry about. Michele was anxious about every medical checkup, followed by concerns about her own health as well. Flooded with anxiety, unaccustomed to dealing independently with her feelings, Michele became temporarily irrational. Any time she or Jenny got a cough or cold, her anxiety made her start to worry that both of them had been infected with terrible illnesses.

The last straw was, of all things, the annual termite inspection at her house. She did indeed have a termite infestation that required immediate treatment with the standard chemicals used for that purpose. Michele panicked. The termite treatment, she feared, would cause brain damage to herself and her daughter. On the other hand, if she didn't have it done, her house would be eaten away. Again, a decision had to be made.

Facing the fear, Michele did her research and decided to treat the outside and her garage only. She explored which chemicals were least toxic and chose a termite control company that used the safest type of insecticide. And finally, she and her daughter went to live with her aunt for a few days while the treatment was being done.

Michele discovered that, having problem-solved to her own satisfaction, she reduced this particular panic and added to her list of independently solved problems. Beginning with her decision to adopt, and continuing decision by decision, each time she solved a problem on her own, she reduced the level of panic and anxiety she faced the next time. It became clear to Michele that there was light at the end of this pattern-breaking tunnel. If she kept breaking her pattern, and kept building her skills and confidence, she would be able to have the satisfactions of motherhood without the anxiety.

Hardest and Best Thing I've Ever Done

Michele broke her pattern. Using the *breaking by letting go* technique she gave up the comforts that the pattern provided and, in time, was able to exchange those limited comforts for much greater rewards—the fulfillment of motherhood and the satisfaction of making good decisions both for herself and for Jenny Lee.

In the end, Michele adjusted to the routine of single working motherhood, and tamed her anxieties. She developed new competencies and learned to rely on her own judgment and abilities as never before. She built on each small success and grew in her competence as a strong and loving mother.

According to Michele, when she looked back on her use of the SUBGAP method to give up her pattern so she could become a mom, "It was the *hardest* thing I've ever done, and it was the *best* thing I've ever done."

Can You Let Go?

As you saw in the case of Michele, breaking your patterns also means leaving some of the perks of those patterns behind. One of those perks is the complaisance that develops when you live a certain way for a long time. True, living that way could be robbing you of your fulfillment. But the status quo is "safe," even if it is not what you desire and it offers few unexpected surprises.

If your pattern provides you with some enticements, then to break your pattern, you have to be willing to leave your comfort zone and tolerate growing pains. You have to be willing to move on and leave no forwarding address. The weighing process of the *breaking by letting go* technique will prepare you to do this.

The expression "no pain, no gain" is certainly true when it comes to breaking patterns. The discomfort or jitters or "butterflies in your stomach" is equivalent to what you may have felt on the first day in a new school, or the first time you took a tennis or golf lesson, or stepped off a plane in a country you never visited before. There may be times when your discomfort makes you back away from breaking your pattern even after you have broken it a few times already. Don't be hard on yourself about it. Letting go takes some getting used to.

Taking It Slowly

If the divorce from your old patterns is too much to handle all at once, I think it is important to remember to practice "moderation in all things" as the ancient Roman playwright

Terence recommended. *Breaking by letting go* is something you have to build up to. You have to use a weighing process for a period of time. You can only make that final leap to breaking your pattern when your daily comparing process is complete and you are ready.

At times, your pattern may seem to be stronger than you are. Don't be discouraged. It is important to approach the pattern-breaking process in ways that are *do-able* for you. A growing collection of positive outcomes will encourage you to go further.

Be aware that some discomforts may occur in your period of adjustment to life immediately after pattern breaking. Take heart. Once you adjust and develop the competencies you need to live a more fulfilled life, the discomforts *will* pass.

Michele found something in her life that inspired her enough to risk leaving the comfort zone that her pattern provided. You can, too.

As filmmaker George Lucas said, "You have to find something that you love enough to be able to take those risks, to be able to jump over the hurdles, to be able to break through the brick walls that are always going to be placed in front of you."

When you break your pattern by letting go of the perks it provided, you can gain a life filled with rewards you never imagined possible. The "something" worth taking a risk to obtain is the reward of living an unpatterned life that is true to yourself and expressive of your potential!

PART FIVE

Guarding Against Patterns

—✎—

We are what we repeatedly do.
Excellence, then, is a habit.

—Socrates

CHAPTER 16

Guard It with Your Lifestyle

～

IMAGINE THAT YOU went on a diet and exercise program, and you achieved your target weight and fitness level. Would that mean that you would never have to think about your diet or exercise again? Of course not. As a matter of fact, if you took that attitude you'd be out of shape again relatively quickly.

A similar rule applies to breaking your patterns. Once you've broken your unproductive pattern, you do indeed have cause for celebration. But, you can't relax your vigilance forever after. Your work is not over.

It is important to remember that, just as they say in Alcoholics Anonymous, you are never a "recovered" pattern-a-holic; when you've broken your pattern, you'll be a "recovering" pattern-a-holic.

Your life is precious and it is well worth protecting against the bad influence of patterns. So, don't put your pattern-breaking knowledge into the attic. You are going to need to remember all you learned in the previous steps of the pattern-breaking process to develop a full-time Pattern-Proof Mind-Set to keep you safely on the path of fulfilling your potential.

The last step of the SUBGAP method is actually more than just a step that occurs in one moment in time, it is a commitment to adopting a healthy living *practice* and applying it each and every day for the rest of your life. The culmination of the SUBGAP method requires learning the fine art of *guarding against patterns* as an integral part of your daily mindset.

An Effortless Effort

When it comes to *guarding against patterns,* practice really does make perfect. As with any skill you practice, maintaining a Pattern-Proof Mind-Set may take more attention at first, but as you go along you'll soon find that you will be able to maintain it with surprisingly little attention. Keeping your unproductive patterns at bay requires a very small investment. It's important to keep your objective in mind—namely, a lifetime that is free from the control of your patterns. So if you want a lifetime during which you fulfill your potential, don't leave out this final step.

Once you master this last step of the SUBGAP method, *guarding against patterns* (the GAP in SUBGAP) will simply become a *permanent* part of the process of living your life to your fullest potential.

The goal is to make sure that no pattern can ever hold you back. Guarding against your pattern means that no pattern gets a chance to entrap you before your Pattern-Proof Mind-Set navigates you past it. The Pattern-Proof Mind-Set is, in effect, a form of enlightenment. It achieves a state of mind that continues to maintain an awareness of your patterns, is alert to the signs that your pattern may be arising, and smoothly sidesteps them—without much effort.

Guarding against patterns is a two-pronged process. You have to master the Pattern-Proof Mind-Set and you have to stay committed to *practicing* this mindset—not just for the short-term but for the rest of your life. *You can never take your patternless life for granted!*

Now, let's look at how to develop and maintain a lifelong and relatively effortless Pattern-Proof Mind-Set.

CHAPTER 17

The Pattern-Proof Mind-Set

~

ONCE YOU HAVE broken your pattern for the first time, the experience of how it feels to live in an unpatterned way becomes permanently embedded inside you. The experience of living free of your patterns is now part of you, and the feeling of expanded possibilities for your life is certain. Nothing can take the knowledge of this experience away from you. And once you are living up to your potential, you'll want to maintain that experience for as long as you live.

But there is something that could make your fulfilling new unpatterned experience take a backseat—*a relapse.*

I wish I could tell you that once you have gotten good at breaking your patterns you will be permanently immune to their influence and never be in danger of falling under their influence again. But I can't.

Through the successful use of the SUBGAP method, you accomplish the *deactivation* of your unproductive patterns so that you can make better and more successful choices. But those well-worn pathways of your old unproductive patterns haven't been surgically removed from your psyche; they can't be. Therefore, there is the danger that they can be reactivated and you could potentially slip under their control again.

Even if I can't promise you the moon, the real story is still pretty darn good. Instead of a miracle cure for patterns that erases them so that you never have to worry about them again, the next best thing is a strategy to make them a non-issue for you for the rest of your life.

Your Life Preserver

The way the human mind is constructed—in combination with the demands of life these days—means that there is no passive solution to remaining free from unproductive patterns. You can't just learn how to break your unproductive patterns and then coast along for the rest of your life.

Why not?

Because, if you forget you ever had an unproductive pattern in the first place, which is easy to do once you become accustomed to success, you are likely to let your guard down. After months or even years without a recurrence you might find yourself thinking, "Why can't I just relax about my patterns? I haven't had a problem with them for a long time!"

Or your thinking might go like this: "If patterns haven't bothered me for a while, maybe they are permanently gone and I don't have to ever give them another thought."

It's a very uplifting but *false* assumption. Similar confidence was expressed in a press release by the vice president of the White Star Line, Philip A. S. Franklin, when he heard that his premier ship had just hit an iceberg back on the morning of April 15, 1912. He said, "We place absolute confidence in the *Titanic*. We believe that the boat is unsinkable."

Your pattern-free life is *not* unsinkable. You must learn how to take the proper precautions.

Don't ever forget that your unproductive patterns were a part of your life for a long, long time, and that means they have the power of old habits to show up again. Relax your vigilance, and they're almost sure to kick you when you're down, precisely when you want them the least. They'll try to take back control at times of change—for instance, when you're in a new situation, facing new challenges, in a new relationship, or a new job, or a new neighborhood.

Unproductive patterns will try to sneak in when you are blue, when you are running a fever or overtired, when you are coping with a disappointment or saddened by a loss. They'll attempt to get your life under their influence again when the deadlines get tight or when you're struggling with a tough decision. The old pattern will then have an opportunity to take over. Your unproductive patterns could even sneak up on you when you are heady with good fortune, a marriage, a new baby, or a career success.

So how do you stay free and clear of your patterns? The answer is, by developing the Pattern-Proof Mind-Set.

Becoming "Pattern-Proof"

Guarding against patterns doesn't mean you have to walk on pins and needles or be constantly wary. But it does mean that you have to install an alarm system inside yourself that is constantly ready to sound a warning when an intrusion by patterns is being attempted. Upon receiving that warning, you have to be alert. Once in a while, that "alarm" will go off, and you'll know you have to do a quick sidestep to insure that your life remains pattern-proof. *Guarding against patterns* is a way of *practicing mastery* over your life on a full-time basis.

Maintaining mindful awareness about your patterns can become a daily practice. You may find it a bit of a challenge to learn but, once it is a regular part of your routine, it is something you'll do happily every day. After you get some experience with *guarding against* your patterns, you will even look forward to doing it.

Take morning exercise. Everybody grumbles about it at first. But if you do it regularly, eventually it becomes a part of your routine. Sooner or later the positive benefits of that practice become clear to you and you start to enjoy and look forward to that part of your life.

When you've guarded against your patterns for some time, you will enjoy immensely the benefits to your life. You will relish the enhanced ability to accomplish your goals and fulfill your potential that comes along with your freedom from unproductive patterns. Imagine feeling ready—as you wake every morning—to "seize the day," as wrote Roman philosopher Horace.

But you will also need *daily practice;* the Pattern-Proof Mind-Set requires that you really do practice being ready every day to meet the challenge. You have to be ready to sound the alarm and boot patterns out of your life before they even get inside the door.

There are three forms of sensors in the *guarding against patterns* alarm system that make up the Pattern-Proof Mind-Set:

1. **Situational Awareness.** *You practice paying a light level of attention to the external situations that could stimulate your pattern.*

2. **Action and Consequence Awareness.** *You practice remaining slightly on alert to which of your actions and their consequences could signal the fact that you are heading down a patterned path.*

3. ***Awareness of Thoughts, Feelings, and Intuitions.***
   You practice maintaining a lightly observing "third eye" on your thoughts, feelings, and intuitions that can help you tell if you are living in a patterned or unpatterned way.

By the time you have reached the *guarding against patterns* step, you know what a warning of your pattern looks like and feels like, and how that differs from the look and feel of your unpatterned living. Therefore, only a lightly applied awareness is necessary.

It would be equivalent to knowing what a mouse looks like scurrying across your kitchen floor, and knowing also that the mouse doesn't belong in your house. That is, you don't need to have a very high level of alertness to notice the mouse in the first place. You know that your preferred kitchen residents include your dog and your two cats—so the mouse stands out as an intruder. You could then take appropriate measures to eliminate the rodent.

The point is, you know what belongs in your kitchen and what doesn't. Once you can see and understand your patterns, you know what belongs in your life and what doesn't. So it doesn't take much attention to notice when something is amiss. Once you notice, you can upgrade your attention level until the potential problem is eliminated. Then, when the immediate danger has passed, you can scale back down to lightly maintaining awareness until the next alert.

Situational Awareness

The first, and simplest, alertness practice in the Pattern-Proof Mind-Set is noticing when you are in a situation that might stimulate your pattern. Even after you have broken your pattern, if you know the kind of situation in which your unproductive pattern had taken over your functioning in the past, you can make arrangements to ensure that every upcoming situation of that kind will be *pattern resistant*.

For instance, say you know that your unproductive pattern tended to occur in your work life, and you have discovered that it usually came out when you were talking with your boss. Perhaps you've discovered that, in meetings with your boss, you had a tendency to react impulsively. When you heard a criticism coming your way, you gave in to a knee-jerk reflex to defend yourself immediately rather than thinking through your response. You noticed that this pattern led to an unpleasant discussion that made your boss feel like blaming you for whatever problem was being discussed.

If you followed the SUBGAP method, perhaps you broke this pattern several times using the *tao of pattern breaking* approach. You discovered that if you did nothing after a criticism, and reviewed your thoughts instead, you could speak less defensively and the meeting went much better. At first, you really had to fight your impulse to defend yourself as every fiber of your being wanted to justify your actions—it was hard to bite your tongue. But by holding your ground against the pattern, the impulse to participate in it passed.

As you accrue a number of successes in breaking your pattern in meetings of this kind, can you just forget about the problem and assume you are past it? Of course not! What if your meetings with your boss went well for six months—could you forget about it then? No, not even then.

Now, how do you *keep* this pattern broken? How do you *guard against* your defensive stance with your boss and clear the way for smooth sailing at work from now on?

You might suppose you have to be on your guard every second, but that's not so. There is a middle ground between the great struggle that your first few breaking successes may have required, and having a completely carefree attitude.

The preventive measure is what I have described as "increased situational awareness"—and it can be relatively effortless. Just put up your antennae in the situation that used to stimulate your pattern to control you. And, for good measure, stay alert in situations that are similar to the one that used to stimulate your pattern. If you are on alert, even on a low-level alert, it is easier and quicker to get into gear if you have to pull out a pattern-breaking technique and nip your pattern in the bud. Now let's look at how to go about putting a full-time *protective cushion* between yourself and your patterns—how to create a situational *buffer*.

Situational Buffering

Once you have identified a pattern-stimulating situation in your life, applying a preventive procedure every time you enter into that situation can serve as a buffer against your pattern's control.

For instance, in the pattern of defensiveness with the boss I just described, say you discover that starting off with small talk about news or sports, even for a minute or two, breaks the ice and creates an atmosphere in which the pattern is less likely to occur. You could regularly apply that approach. Or you could apply the business adage of making sure you talk only 30 percent of the time and let the boss talk 70 percent of the time as insurance against that defensive pattern showing.

Applying such *buffering* tactics in a formerly pattern-provoking situation does several good things. Buffering tactics increase the "cushion" zone between your vibrant patternless living and your restrictive patterned life; they buy you lead time to warn you in advance to wake up and smell the coffee so you are ready to defend your more fulfilled life from threat; they provide you with simple tactics you can put into daily practice that can keep you in control of your direction in the face of threats that your pattern wants to regain control.

If you apply buffering tactics, the situation will unfold differently than it would have when your pattern was in control.

Of course, the simplest way to act on your situational

awareness and the most effective buffer would be to avoid that pattern-provoking situation altogether. But how often is that a realistic solution? Very rarely. Since patterns tend to be interwoven with our daily lives, it is impossible or impractical to completely avoid situations that stimulated patterns in the past.

Action and Consequence Awareness

With a "guarding-against" mind-set, in addition to being alert to the situations that warn you about your pattern, you can also keep aware of your own actions, as well as the reactions from others, that have in the past been associated with your unproductive pattern. In using *action and consequence awareness,* rather than using the *situation* to alert you, you are relying on cues from your own behavior and the behavior of others to tell you when your pattern may be planning to try to take back control of your life.

In the process of *seeing, understanding,* and *breaking* your pattern, you get to know your pattern very well indeed. Then you get familiar with the behaviors—the action steps—that go along with that pattern. If you notice yourself participating in one of these behaviors, it can serve as a red flag.

After you have done a thorough analysis of your pattern in daily life, you also know just what reactions and consequences you tend to receive from the world when you participate in your pattern. Remain mindful about whether or not you are receiving one of those reactions, since noticing it can also serve as a red flag.

Take a Cue from Yourself

Suppose you have learned through the SUBGAP process that you have an unproductive pattern of arguing with authority figures at times when you need their cooperation or help. Say you know from past experience that these patterned disputes always end up undercutting your chances to advance yourself in school, at work, or in a community organization. If you know that your pattern had a tendency to reveal itself through arguments with authority, and if you know that when it played out, it always cost you dearly, you can commit to "staying tuned" when you're disagreeing with anyone who's in charge.

If you notice yourself starting to disagree with what you are hearing, or notice yourself presenting facts to the contrary, you know there is a good chance that your pattern (and its ill effects) are not far behind. Likewise, say you notice a critical or contradictory reaction from someone who is in charge and has some control over your destiny. You need to consider the possibility that this can be signaling the imminent onset of your pattern.

Don't wait for absolute proof—by then it will be too

late! Remain alert. Take the hint from your own actions and the reactions of others. Learn to glimpse these red flags the moment you see them.

Buffering Actions and Consequences

Once an action or consequence raises a red flag—and before your pattern has any chance of rearing its ugly head—you can apply buffering tactics to provide a cushioning zone that keeps you safe. Again, let's look at guarding against an unproductive pattern of arguing with authority. In a discussion, you notice yourself disagreeing with someone in charge. A simple buffer would be to wind down the discussion and find a reason to postpone its resumption until you are ready to reapproach it safely.

Are you concerned about being too careful and not speaking up for yourself? Don't worry. If, after careful evaluation, you later decide that you were behaving in your own best interest and it was *not* an example of your pattern, you can usually go back and argue further at a future point.

On the other hand, say you have an unproductive pattern of sheepishly complying with authority when it is in your best interest to stand up for yourself, and a pattern of kicking yourself later for that. You notice yourself participating in the action of smiling and politely agreeing with instructions that seem off base to you. In this case, remaining alert to your own smiling and agreeing allows you to use those actions as a signal that your pattern of compliance might be close at hand. It allows you to know when to take a look at exactly what you are acquiescing to so that you apply a buffer between the action you noticed and the onset of your pattern. In this case you might decide, as a matter of course whenever you notice yourself smiling and agreeing, to ask for more clarification of the questionable directive, so that you can better evaluate whether to beg to differ. No harm in asking a question, and that buffer will put you in a better position to sidestep your pattern.

The red-flag response tells you to do a quick self-check and take the measure of your own actions and the reactions you're getting from others. Applying a buffer when that red flag goes up buys you time or creates some distance between your red flag action and the unfurling of your pattern. Better yet, it creates a change of pace and reduces the chance your pattern will erupt. By using *action and consequence awareness* along with some buffering activity, your pattern doesn't have a chance to get off the ground.

Awareness of Thoughts, Feelings, and Intuitions

Whereas *action and consequence awareness* focuses on your outward behavior and the behavior of others, you can also *guard against patterns* using what I call an "inner barometer" that measures whether you are on a path toward your goals or on a path leading you back into your pattern.

What do I mean by inner barometer?

In part, it's your own personal awareness of thoughts, feelings, cravings, temptations, and intuitions that are associated with your pattern. *Awareness of thoughts, feelings, and intuitions* is the third component of a Pattern-Proof Mind-Set.

If your inner barometer warns you about stormy conditions, it should be equally sensitive to fair weather. In other words, your inner experiences can help you sense when you are heading toward a pattern and when you are heading toward your heartfelt goals. These diametrically opposed directions will be accompanied by *very* different internal experiences.

For many, it is an intuition that starts the pattern alert signal. When a pattern is imminent, you might get a "gut feeling" that you're going off track. I've had some people tell me that they felt out of balance or literally felt the hair rise on the back of their necks when their patterns tried to control them. Others describe the feeling as a certain kind of "heaviness" when patterns came back to reassert themselves.

Or there may be a specific thought or feeling that is related to your particular pattern—a thought or feeling you've come to understand through the SUBGAP process. Or maybe you'll notice that you feel doubtful, or nervous, or impatient, or disappointed, or weighed down if you are heading back under the control of your pattern. For instance, one of my patients reported that, nine times out of ten, feeling "disappointed" was a reliable signal that her pattern was trying to take over her life. Another reported that when he felt something was "unfair," it was a pretty good indicator that his pattern was attempting to make an entrance into his life.

Whatever the reaction, people who have been guarding against their patterns for some time report that they have one set of inner experiences when they are on the right track to success and another set of inner experiences when they are in danger of slipping into an unproductive pattern.

I've found that people who have successfully been through the SUBGAP method and have broken their patterns are usually able to tell the difference between the inner experiences that went along with their pattern and the inner experiences that go along with pattern-free living. For example, maybe you'll have a sense of wholeness, or feel proud of yourself, or feel compassionate toward someone else, or happy with your progress when you are on the right track. These are the kinds of positive feelings associated with having broken your pattern.

You really will be able to *tell the difference* between pattern-related thoughts, feelings, and intuitions, and those that are associated with living up to your potential. The difference between the two inner states of being can be as clear as the difference between night and day. Being mindful of these two contrasting experiences can be instrumental in maintaining your Pattern-Proof Mind-Set and keeping yourself on course.

Let Your Inner Barometer Be Your Guide

The buffering tactics that you can use in response to practicing *awareness of thoughts, feelings, and intuitions* are a more subtle part of the Pattern-Proof Mind-Set.

Letting your inner barometer be a guide for creating a buffer zone against patterns works like this: When you get a red flag signaling a thought or emotion that was once associated with your pattern, you add a cushioning zone against your pattern by changing course. You can adjust what you are saying, what you are doing, or you can remove yourself from a situation altogether. Your inner red flag tells you when it is time to turn away from what you are saying or doing at any moment—and you can keep correcting your course until you are outside of the range of your pattern's control.

When your inner barometer returns to thoughts and feelings associated with your unpatterned lifestyle, you know you have corrected course and successfully sidestepped the danger of falling into your unproductive pattern. Using your inner experience as a guide, you will be able to tell that you are out of danger when your red flag thought or emotion subsides and your inner barometer no longer warns of an impending storm.

Guarding Against Patterns: Case of the Guilt Barometer

Let's look at the case of Sally, a high-powered concert promoter who came to talk with me when panic attacks started to take over her life. The problem started to become debilitating when she found herself hesitant to attend the meetings and social events required to do her job. What held her back was fear that she would experience an attack.

An operational understanding of her pattern suggested that, whenever she felt that a client or co-worker was behaving unprofessionally, she had a difficult time confronting that person and became very anxious. For instance, one of her employees kept asking a star for his autograph during a business meeting instead of concentrating on the backstage requirements. Sally knew the employee was out of line and felt embarrassed by the whole situation.

Sally didn't want to complain, and she worried about upsetting her employee or, worse yet, getting that employee into trouble. Consequently, she never said a word about the incident. However, she was afraid to go into work the next day because she felt very anxious. Indeed, she did have a panic attack driving into work and had to pull over her car so she wouldn't crash.

As Sally came to a historical understanding of her problem, she linked her present guilt feelings to a time in her teens when her relationship with her mother was extremely tense. Sally refused to overlook her father's misbehavior, even though her mother said it "broke her heart" every time Sally made an issue of it. But how could she ignore the behavior of a man who left his family sitting outside in the car for an hour or two while he had a few drinks with his bar buddies on the way to or from any family event? Yet whenever Sally had been angry at her father for misbehaving, her mother begged Sally to forgive him.

Sally would feel guilty for upsetting her mother. Eventually, she'd relent and let each incident pass. Soon, like her mother, she learned to pretend that everything was "perfectly normal"—even when they were sitting in the car waiting for her father to come out of the bar.

Sally learned to see her pattern of getting upset, becoming guilty, feeling thwarted in her ability to correct situations, and then panicking. She was able to use the rapid correction method to break this pattern by taking an action to address the problem, but in a quiet and nonconfrontational way— by e-mail. When she wanted to speak up, she did it quietly and immediately found that she could effectively make her point and set people straight by e-mail communication rather than in-person confrontation.

The more Sally spoke up for herself instead of pretending that things were fine, the fewer panics she experienced. But her track record was far from perfect. She still had some panic attacks, and her pattern was still drawing her in from time to time. How could she get better at guarding against her pattern?

The Guilty Signal

Sally became aware that guilt was the main feeling state associated with her patterned way of living. She felt guilty about speaking up for herself or for speaking up on behalf of the project she was promoting at the moment, if it meant that someone else would be upset that things weren't going to seem "perfectly normal." Sally learned that she could heighten her inner awareness of that guilt feeling and use it as a cue to be mindful that something was not perfectly normal and had to be corrected. Her guilt was a reliable indicator that she was about to overlook something, about to begin her pattern and risk a panic attack.

After one of her colleagues accompanied Sally to a studio in which a TV commercial for an upcoming event was being filmed, Sally ended up feeling guilty and she didn't quite know why. What she did know, from her historical understanding, was that this guilt was probably a feeling associated with patterned things and *not* with her true self. The guilt feeling alerted Sally to the threat of falling under the control of her pattern. It was in stark contrast to her otherwise unpatterned freedom to do what was best for each concert promotion, netting her the reputation of "Queen of Concerts."

Sally had learned to take her inner barometer very seriously and rather than simply viewing her inner experience as nothing more than a feeling, she saw it as a cue to the possible arrival of her pattern. So she reviewed the events of the day. She realized that she was a little upset with her colleague's attempts to make himself the contact for their agency after Sally had already established a good relationship with the artist and her agency. Sally immediately corrected the situation by e-mail. Had she not used her guilt as a guide, things might have gone on longer, her feelings might have grown, and panics could have occurred before a correction was made.

The more Sally heeded to this cue, the less she fell into her patterned panic. As her life became more patternless, even the incidences of feeling guilty reduced until months would pass between guilt feelings. But when they did arrive they were inevitably a heads up to pay attention to her impending pattern.

But What If?

How will you feel when, despite your best efforts, you slip into an old pattern? It is not a disaster if you relapse. If you fall into your unproductive pattern and participate in it again, don't panic. Don't be too hard on yourself.

Even with your most diligent pattern-breaking and

guarding-against efforts, you might relapse anyway. That does not mean that all of your efforts have been in vain. It is good to be competent at getting right back on the horse that threw you. Part of guarding against patterns is the ability to quickly and efficiently recover from a relapse.

Simply return to the relevant step of the SUBGAP method. In most cases, you don't have to go back to square one, since your ability to *see* and *understand* your pattern should remain intact. Typically, you might have to return to the *breaking* step, and practice that again. Then, after enough successes, move back into *guarding against patterns.*

However, there will be times when you do have to backtrack a bit, and you will have to reapply a top-down and bottom-up analysis of your life while reapplying the SUBGAP method. This is especially important to remember when life circumstances change since this can muddy the waters and throw new elements into the mix. When your surroundings or the usual people around you change, it is often difficult to see how your pattern is elbowing its way into your life.

If your guarding-against awareness is picking up some red flags, and you are in new circumstances when this happens, you may have to review the nitty-gritty details of those new circumstances to get your bearings. When you see and understand how your pattern is trying to control you in the new conditions, then you can return to the *breaking* step and continue from there.

I assure you, the longer you use the SUBGAP method, the easier and faster the process becomes and the more likely you are to arrive at a fulfilling pattern-proof lifestyle in the end. Once you know how to break and *guard against patterns,* that knowledge becomes a permanent part of you. Then, even if you temporarily forget (and relapse into your pattern), you have it in you to get back on track and curtail your pattern with relatively little effort.

Thomas Jefferson said, "The price of freedom is eternal vigilance." When you consider the liberating benefits, you will certainly agree that the vigilance required to *guard against patterns* is a small price to pay for the success and fulfillment of your unpatterned life.

PART SIX

Patterned and Unpatterned Life

～

*Be glad of life because it gives you the chance
to love and to work
and to play and to look up at the stars.*

—Henry Van Dyke

CHAPTER 18

Patterns at Work

⁓

AFTER DECADES OF using psychoanalytic principles to help coach business people in my office, it is quite clear to me that success in the work world is the sum total of two, and only two, equally important factors:

1. *Successfully accomplishing your assigned work projects and tasks.*
2. *Successfully managing your work relationships and politics.*

Sometimes these two factors go hand-in-hand and sometimes they work against each other. Balancing these two factors in the work world is the formula for career success. However, such a balancing act between task and people skills requires paying good attention to the tasks while also attending to the personalities and politics.

In both of these key areas, advancement in your career requires the same ability to take advantage of opportunities and avoid pitfalls. This is generally true no matter what profession you choose, what type of work you do, whether you work for a large corporation or a small mom-and-pop shop or run your own business.

Occasionally, you might find a work environment in which doing a good job is enough to advance, or others in which being a good politician alone will do the trick, but, for the most part, a healthy portion of both capacities is the formula for success. If unproductive patterns hold you back from excelling in the task-oriented side or the people-skills side, or both, you might find that your career is an area in which you are experiencing underfulfillment.

The work world is fast-paced and competitive. There is no room for patterns that interfere with your ability to read and respond to the politics and personalities. There is also no room for patterns that interfere with your doing your best at the tasks you set about to accomplish in your job. If you can do a good job and conduct yourself well in work-world politics and among different personalities, you'll be more likely to accomplish your goals as well as to be recognized and appreciated and advance your career.

If you feel that you have the potential to do better but

aren't doing your best work, or that you have the potential to be more advanced in terms of your position, compensation, or recognition, it could be that patterns are holding you back in one or both of the work world's requirements for success.

Managing Patterns in Work Relationships

Let's look at the patterns in the politics and personalities side of business. Because the structure of work-world relationships is hierarchical, with assigned positions, this creates a common set of situationally induced patterns. The hierarchy, the fact that you have a boss or supervisor, automatically puts you in a junior position to that person. Likewise, the fact that you manage an employee or staff member automatically puts you in a senior position in relation to them. Psychoanalysts believe that this can set the stage for parent-child patterns to show themselves in all their variations and permutations.

In such a pattern, you might unwittingly start to behave as if you are the child and your boss or manager is the adult. For instance, you begin to look for approval or help from a boss simply because that person is senior to you. Once you are participating in a childish type of pattern, it is easy to forget to notice whether or not your boss or employee is really ready, willing, and able to parent you.

Some indications of a childish pattern in employees is a

feeling of fear of the superior, a feeling of rebelliousness against the person, or an overly helpless, sluggish, procrastinating, or dependent attitude toward him or her.

Just because someone is above you in the hierarchy doesn't mean that her or she is more mature or more together than you. Sometimes that person is, but sometimes not. If your boss is less mature, or less together, then your expectations and behavior toward your senior has to take this into account.

If your unproductive pattern induces you to look toward a less mature boss for approval, or toward a less competent boss for help, things are going to run into trouble. Additionally, just because someone is a manager or a boss doesn't mean that that person is immune to his or her own patterns.

As an employee, you have very few options other than to learn how to overcome your own work-world-related patterns and how to operate successfully, taking into account the work-related patterns of your supervisors. Applying the SUBGAP method to overcoming your work patterns will help you to more successfully manage your boss, so that, as management guru Peter Drucker said, "He becomes your resource for achievement."

Managing to Manage

If you are a manager at work, responsibilities and people and project challenges are increased since you are faced with not only your own productivity, but the productivity of those you manage. One might think that, as a manager, you have more options at your disposal than you would as a more junior employee. After all, if an employee doesn't take advantage of chances to get with the program, possibly that employee can be replaced. But usually, as a manager, you will be required to first try to make the situation work.

Just because you manage other employees, it doesn't mean that they are oriented toward following your instructions. You can't assume that they consider you a more knowledgeable person from whom they could be learning a thing or two.

As a manager, unproductive patterns might lead you to act as if you are a parent and your staff members are children. Some indications of a parental-type pattern in managers is feeling impatience, looking down on subordinates, cleaning up after subordinates, or being overly helpful, micro-managing, lecturing, or even having a punitive attitude toward the employees.

As you can see, it can get pretty tricky negotiating the politics of the corporate hierarchy, the realities of who is assigned to report to whom, along with the realities of who is actually mature or a cooperative team player or knowledgeable or skilled, and who is not. It takes a clear eye to notice, accurately read, and successfully navigate all of these interpersonal aspects of the work world. If you are participating in unproductive patterns and add this to the mix, how can you possibly see all the elements clearly and manage your relationships in the work world?

Managing Your Career

Unproductive patterns can be everywhere, and no one is immune. Odds are that many of the other people around you, both your managers and employees, are likely to be a mixed bag of their best side and their unproductive patterns, just like you are.

Success in today's business world is challenging enough in the best of circumstances. Any additional challenges caused by unproductive patterns affecting your work performance or your work relationships could easily become all-consuming. You might forget that, as a businessperson, there are two distinct businesses that you are always required to manage well:

1. *The business of accomplishing the goals that fulfill your part in the overall team success of your company.*
2. *The business of advancing your career and building your own reputation as a successful business person.*

Hollywood actors have agents who manage their careers. Those agents help build a résumé, promote the actors' reputation for success, and negotiate to increase their earning power. In business you have to be your own agent. To succeed, you have to consider not only your task at the moment for the team you are on right now, but also the bigger picture of your own career management over your work-lifetime. As the following examples show, breaking unproductive work patterns can help you accomplish both.

Patterns in Work Politics: The Case of the Golden Rule

Vicky is an extremely dedicated, hardworking, and loyal employee. She is an expert in transportation and large freight shipping, by air, train, boat, and truck. Want to ship a twenty-two-ton marine turbine engine? Need to get it from Oslo, Norway, to Kyoto, Japan, by Wednesday? Can't wait to get a forty-foot-long freight container filled with Ipe deck-building wood from the port of Paranagua, Brazil, to Los Angeles? Vicky will tell you the best, fastest, cheapest way to do so in seconds flat.

Vicky was hired by a very well-known multinational company that shipped heavy mechanical equipment all over the world; and the shipments numbered in the thousands per day from numerous manufacturing and warehousing locations located across three continents. Her assignment was to ensure that each manufacturing division revamped their shipping methods in accordance with her recommendations.

During conventions, meetings, and trade fairs, Vicky had steadily expanded her range of contacts over the years. As a matter of fact, she was on the board of many shipping and trade associations, and an officer in some. In hiring her, the company was relying on Vicky and her strong international network to help save millions of dollars. She was told that results were expected within a two-year period.

Although she began her new job with very high hopes, she quickly discovered that her immediate boss was undercutting her ability to carry out her duties. For instance, her boss instructed Vicky to resign from several of the trade and transportation associations to which she belonged to save on membership fees, airfare to the meetings, and hotel costs.

This would, of course, cripple Vicky's ability to carry out her greater cost-savings goals. She refused to believe that her boss understood the ramifications of this action. To set the record straight, she spent week after week presenting evidence that supported the greater savings that could be obtained by continued involvement and participation in these groups.

Vicky could not accept the possibility that her boss was willing to do the company a disservice. She simply believed that presenting more information would make him see the light. Nonetheless, despite Vicky's persistent arguments, her boss would not budge.

Then Vicky proposed that two of the manufacturing

divisions contract in concert with a certain freight service instead of separately, a plan that would create a total net savings of a half-million dollars in only six months. She was shocked to discover that the two divisions in question overruled her recommendation. They preferred to keep their vendor contracts unchanged and simply renew.

Seeing the Barriers

Vicky did not have the corporate authority to insist upon divisional cooperation. Only her boss's boss, a senior vice president, had that authority, and Vicky had no access to that corporate officer. Her boss, however, did have access. But when Vicky expressed concern that substantial cost savings were about to be lost if the transportation contracts were not renegotiated in time, her boss declined Vicky's request that she go to the vice president. Instead, Vicky's boss blamed her for not being convincing enough to engender the support she needed from the two division heads.

Taking her boss's criticisms to heart, Vicky actually began to feel that she indeed was the failure that her boss portrayed. At her six-month review, she was told that her performance in cost-savings was not anywhere near what was expected. She was warned that this had to change or her position might be eliminated.

Vicky became very upset and lost total confidence in her

own abilities. She became withdrawn and felt totally defeated. She was nervous about talking to her boss or about presenting at any meetings. At this point, she consulted with me about her situation.

As I listened to Vicky's story, it became apparent to me that her boss was participating in a pattern of undermining Vicky's ability to carry out her assignment. But Vicky *did not see it*. It had never occurred to her, even for a moment, that her boss was undercutting her. Vicky believed that if the corporate goals were met and the additional savings were accomplished, the tightening of the corporate belt would stop and everyone would benefit. She couldn't understand why her boss wouldn't support her efforts to do her job. She believed her boss when he said that the fault lay with her.

Ruled by the Golden Rule

Many good, decent, team-spirited, ethical corporate employees are undone by a pattern of assuming that just because they are behaving in the best interest of the corporate goals, all others in the company are oriented to behave that way, too. Vicky was subject to this common pattern and believed, "If I'm a certain way, then others must be that way, too."

This pattern at work is a variation on the theme of the Golden Rule. The Golden Rule states that a person should, "Do unto others as you would have others do unto you."

Many people who follow the Golden Rule also assume that if you treat others the way you want to be treated, then those others will return the favor and treat you properly as well. Good people have a hard time believing this is not always the case. It's a hard pill to swallow when they find that their own good efforts do not inspire others to return the favor.

For Vicky, the situation just did not compute. It was inconceivable to Vicky that her boss might have a personal agenda or pattern of his own that caused this conflict. What was that agenda? Maybe he was insecure. Did he think there was a danger that Vicky would shine too brightly, and his performance would be overshadowed by hers? Or perhaps he felt her performance would undermine his own attempts to progress within the corporation. There was also the possibility that he was making wrong choices because he was simply blinded by a pattern of being "penny wise and pound foolish."

Whatever his agenda, Vicky's boss was undeniably inflicting damage on her performance and, quite possibly, undermining her career. He consistently neglected to *even mention* Vicky's plan of combining the divisional shipping contracts to the vice president. But Vicky's pattern was to try hard, believe only the best about others, and to believe that, if there was a failure along the line, somehow it was her own fault. In a corporate setting this good-intentioned but rather naive pattern can be professionally suicidal.

Course Correction

Since she could not *see* what was happening, Vicky couldn't correct it. She started to despair that she would ever get her job done.

Upon exploring the nitty-gritty details of her work situation, it was pretty clear to Vicky that the area of the underachievement was related to her relationship with her boss. A top-down analysis didn't reveal any other distinct area of difficulty. Although Vicky first tried to blame herself and her own inability to be "convincing enough" to the divisions, upon a thorough review of her daily work life she realized that she simply didn't have the corporate clout to make the change happen and that she wasn't getting the support of the people who did have clout.

Although Vicky was driven by her pattern to want to see her boss in the best possible light, when she did a very detailed bottom-up analysis of the situation, she had to admit that her boss was undercutting her. She couldn't deny that she was participating in her own unproductive pattern.

An operational understanding of her pattern also helped relieve Vicky of her feeling responsible for the failure in cost-savings since she had identified how her pattern kept her helpless in this situation. She realized that the two obstacles were her pattern's failing approach and her boss's failing agenda, and that the obstacle was not *herself*.

Unpatterned Empowerment

To break her pattern, Vicky had to notice and counteract attempts by her boss to unempower her. When she looked for an inroad to reversing this pattern, she concluded there were two situations where she had an opportunity to make her opinions better known to others in the company—either at meetings or in the context of group e-mails.

She rightfully anticipated that taking such independent action to sidestep her boss would not be easy to pull off without ruffling his feathers. But she knew that she had to try since her current patterned path was not working.

No longer blinded by her pattern, Vicky realized that working things out with her boss was a lost cause. She began to pursue a strategy of engendering support among her company's leaders at corporate and divisional meetings. She took advantage of group e-mails to further her cause, without pointing any fingers, and described the transportation cost savings that would be realized if others embraced her plan. These efforts produced results. She began to obtain the support she needed to carry out her plan.

Simultaneously, now that she realized that her work at this company would always entail a bit of swimming upstream as long as she was to report to her current boss, she also contacted headhunters and began a job search. Given her reputation in the shipping and transportation industry and her high profile in the trade societies and associations, it wasn't long before she was snapped up by another multinational corporation. Aside from getting higher pay, best of all she entered into her new position with a deal that provided her with the support she needed to do her job. It was a deal she negotiated clearly and up front to begin the process of guarding against her pattern in her next career move.

The triumph, for Vicky, was in recognizing and acknowledging that she worked for someone who just didn't fit her patterned view of the world. By realizing that, she was enabled to break her pattern. New flexibility gave her the opportunity to approach the situation in a different way. She discovered a way to make the situation work for her whether others followed the Golden Rule or not.

Where in the Work Are Your Patterns Hiding?

There are so many aspects to succeeding in business these days: managing, negotiating, consensus-building, leadership, cost-containment, analytical skills, selling, marketing, presenting, reporting, communicating, and many more.

The multifaceted skill sets required to succeed and move ahead also provide many inroads for unproductive patterns since, depending upon your own unconscious mind, it is possible for a pattern to take place in one or more of the many areas of business life.

Are your unproductive patterns embedded in your communication style, your management style, your selling abilities, your leadership efforts, your negotiating skills, your detail orientation, or your ability to meet deadlines? Obviously, there is a lot of room for examination.

As difficult as it might be to single out the area that needs most attention—and find the unproductive pattern that could be hurting you—it is well worth the effort. If you shed unproductive patterns at work, you sharply improve your chances of reaching your overall career goals. And in the meantime, you are likely to enhance your ability to achieve success working with your current team on projects that are underway.

A Case of Work Task Patterns: Mitch's Perfect Pitches

Mitch was an extremely creative and talented account manager at a large advertising agency in New York. He first came to see me, in shock, when he had just been *demoted* to assistant account manager.

In his new second-in-command position, he was now required to report to a colleague who had joined the agency four years after him. Needless to say, Mitch was rather distraught at being forced to report to a younger, less experienced account manager.

Mitch was unquestionably "the man" when it came to putting together a brilliant advertising campaign. When companies wanted to "remake" the image of a product, Mitch was known as the guy who could do it. The media and print ads produced on his projects were visions of perfection. He made sure that every *i* was dotted, and every *t* crossed.

Nothing went out until it was perfect. Mitch put in countless late-night hours working out details on these projects. Once he took on a client account, he was literally on a mission and would not rest until the mission was accomplished.

You've probably seen some of his ads, as they are quite memorable. Everybody said so. Still, despite all of this talent, Mitch was demoted. Neither his boss, the creative department people at his agency, nor the clients were happy with him. All admitted that his work was the best they'd seen in ages. But Mitch's perfectionist style created a lot of problems for everyone around him.

The "Glass Ceiling" of Patterns

Laboring long and hard to revise the final versions of his presentations, Mitch was often late for meetings with the client. This left his boss with the uncomfortable responsibility of filling in the blanks until Mitch arrived. Furthermore, his interest in tweaking media and print ads until every detail was perfect frequently caused him to go over-budget.

Creative and media people found themselves pulling out

their hair when working on one of Mitch's campaigns. He called for so many revisions and spent so much time on the fine-detail work, that even the most well-intentioned colleagues began to dread working on projects with him. As a result, Mitch found that the production people began to drag their feet when he called for changes on his projects. Some even began to ignore his requests. This, in turn, made his final product take even longer than before. Instances of lateness and unmet deadlines started to become more noticeable.

Even after several warnings from his boss to move more quickly, Mitch still felt that he could not compromise the quality of the ads. Eventually, his boss was compelled to ask him to provide her with the presentations a day in advance. And because he had showed up late at so many meetings, she would simply meet with the client without Mitch, from then on.

Finally, the situation had simply become untenable. Clearly, that was the reason Mitch was demoted. The less-experienced person who took his place was also less brilliant. But producing a perfect product had to be balanced against the constraints of budgeting and schedule.

Why Me?

Mitch was able to present enough information to outline his pattern clearly, but he did so without seeming to feel that the reactions of others at work were at all justified.

It was clear that the unconscious nature of his pattern—

combined with the Dignity Shield—made it impossible for Mitch to understand why he had been demoted. As we reviewed the events leading up to his demotion, he recalled there had been several warnings. But no matter what his boss said, Mitch felt he was having such great success in his ad campaigns that it was incomprehensible—to him—that his boss, colleagues, and clients would want him to change his ways. After all, he insisted, wasn't the final product all that counted?

Alternately befuddled and angered by his reversal of fortune, Mitch complained, "Didn't they appreciate all the extra hours I spent on those projects? I wasn't hired to work until midnight every night, but I did it anyway and this is the thanks I get!" He felt "stabbed in the back."

Your Patterns or Your Skills?

Although reluctant at first to focus on all the facts, Mitch finally allowed himself to really investigate the nitty-gritty details of this situation thoroughly. It finally became clear to him that his excuses for continuing to drag out the timetables and budgets, even in the face of warnings, did not tell the entire story.

Mitch had to accept the idea of unproductive patterns and the Dignity Shield—that was the only explanation that made sense. Given his attention to detail, he enthusiastically took to the bottom-up analysis of his work life like a fish to water.

Looking at his situation with a scientific eye, Mitch was able to develop an operational understanding of his pattern of perfectionistic behavior. He was simply incompetent at prioritizing the tasks at hand. His pattern's goal was to protect him from feeling incompetent. Instead, he persisted in doing what he did best, and focused on every little nuance—with pride. Consequently, he could not bring himself to pass over details, even if they didn't fit the time-frame or budget.

The simple truth was that Mitch lacked prioritization and time-management skills. His pattern of requiring perfection in every detail prevented him from addressing this deficit in his business abilities. Mitch's perfectionistic pattern had dominated his career and had contributed to both his success and his downfall. It was a double-edged sword. He protested, "I don't want to throw out the baby with the bathwater! What am I going to do when my pattern is my strength and my weakness? I can't give it up!"

But then his operational understanding clicked.

"I can't give it up because I have nothing else to rely on," Mitch realized. It became clear to him that the only way to break his pattern was to learn other skills. He had to devote as much energy to time-management and teamwork skills as he had been giving to perfectionism.

"Yes, I see it now," Mitch admitted with regard to his

pattern. "I need to learn these other skills to break my pattern, but isn't it too late? Isn't my fate already sealed? Why should I even try?"

Second Chances

The answer to Mitch's questions is that careers can take a wrong turn and still recover.

If you understand that unproductive patterns are not a natural part of your system, and if you understand that reinventing yourself as an unpatterned person is always possible, then you know you can develop the skills you need to get more control over your career. True, you have to take steps to break the unproductive pattern, but you have the *tools* to do that.

By using the SUBGAP method and understanding your pattern, you can see where you need to add to your skill set. No matter how long you have participated in your pattern, and no matter how much it has held you back, I want you to know that you can break it and move ahead from *this point onward*.

There is an ancient Chinese saying: "Opportunity is always present in the midst of crisis." This is especially true when it comes to patterns. Sometimes it takes a crisis in order to notice that something is amiss and to rouse you to hunt for an answer. Getting demoted or fired incites just the kind of crisis that also presents an opportunity.

Mitch's career was certainly off track. He had suffered a bad setback. It was very humiliating. But I urged him to use this crisis as an opportunity. It was not irreversible. It was a wake-up call, signaling the presence of an unproductive pattern in his work-task life. Now he had a choice. He didn't have to rely on his pattern. He could use the next period of his career to reinvent himself, to devote himself to learning more about setting priorities, managing his time, and being a better team player.

Understanding his pattern allowed Mitch to see that only by adding these skills could he be perceived of as being reliable, cooperative and a talented master of his profession. And this is what Mitch set out to do.

New and Improved You

Mitch applied the *breaking by letting go* method, so that he could relinquish his perfectionistic pattern as his main source of pride. He realized that he couldn't let go completely without having other important work skills in place to fall back on. So Mitch set out to improve his time-management abilities. He worked with me on exercises and methods to apply at work. He attended numerous weekend seminars on topics related to prioritization, project management, budget, work flow, teamwork, and time management. He also devoted part of every vacation to similar workshops.

Each time he received any work assignment, he was

careful to check the expected delivery date. To guard against his pattern on a daily basis, he worked on a checklist of priority items, a second checklist of items that held secondary importance—and last, a tertiary list of low-importance details.

He began the painstaking task of starting to learn how to estimate how long each task would actually take. Most difficult of all, he forced himself to learn how to cut certain items from the list completely if his budget or time frame did not allow for them.

Eventually, it became clear that he had turned his liability into an asset. His attention to detail—once focused on items of minute importance—now turned to the task of learning and carrying out important new skills.

Before long, Mitch got a lucky break. The colleague who had been promoted to being his boss three years earlier took a maternity leave. Mitch filled in during her absence. It became clear to Mitch's former boss—and to the creative department—that he was a changed man. Deadlines were almost always met. His ad campaigns came in at or under budget. He was suddenly valued as a team player by those he once frustrated.

The way he proved himself increased his property value at the advertising agency. Several months later, when a new account manager slot opened, Mitch was tagged to fill it.

Now, wherever his career took him, as long as he guarded

against the recurrence of his old pattern, his potential could shine. Mitch was back, and he was better than ever.

If *Mitch* could do it, so can you.

If you are being held back in your career by workplace patterns that inhibit either your task or your people skills—imagine the unlimited opportunities ahead if you break through your pattern's "glass ceiling."

CHAPTER 19

Patterns in Love

⁓

IN MY PRACTICE of psychoanalysis, I've listened to people tell me about the highs and lows of their love lives for many years. I hear the same tale oft repeated. As relationships move past the honeymoon stage, people mysteriously find themselves either behaving in a manner they find unbecoming, or tolerating behavior from their partner that they find unacceptable, or both. In either case, the love in the relationship erodes. One of my patients once summed up the mystery of love relationships that become sour and frustrating in this way: "Why do people who are supposed to love each other treat each other like this? It's bizarre!"

The answer to that question is simply that *unproductive relationship patterns* secretly infiltrate into relationships— and not just one person's pattern but often two people's patterns at one time. How could any relationship stand up to this invisible sabotage without suffering some ill effects? As is the case with patterns in all other areas of life, relationship patterns also reside in the unconscious where they secretly erode the love in relationships.

Someone to Love Me for Me

Over the years, I've heard so many people express the idea that they wish to find a partner who will truly accept and love them for "being themselves." I'm sure you have heard this, too. However, it is very important to differentiate here between the two selves that we discussed in light of understanding the "me and not-me" of patterns from chapter 9.

In relationships, the idea of "love me, love my dog" is very pronounced. But, is it realistic to believe that your partner should accept and love you for your true self as well as accept and love your pattern-participating self (especially when your pattern-participating self may cause some relationship trouble)? I think not.

Is it even *loving* of you to impose your unproductive pattern on your partner and expect that partner to handle it well—or for your partner to impose that upon you and expect you to handle it well?

In a true partnership, the goals are to enhance what is good for the partnership and protect the preciousness and joy of that union from whatever threatens it. Over time, if not seen and broken, unproductive patterns can overshadow what is good about a relationship.

The most convincing way to express love is by valuing your relationship with that special person. A realistic way of proving your love is by breaking the unproductive patterns that you impose upon your partner. Isn't this a much more mature expression of love than asking your partner to accept you and your pattern, too? Of course it is.

The Love of Your Life

Two prerequisites to lifelong love have become crystal clear to me:

1. *Finding someone among all the people on this earth who is right for you and with whom the relationship has an original basis in love and attraction.*
2. *Successfully resolving threats to relationship happiness, including and especially unproductive relationship patterns, in order to keep the love alive and the relationship fresh.*

There are different opinions about how many people there are in the world who would be the right partner for you. Some people believe there is only one great love for their lives—the one "right" person—and if they are very lucky they will meet and marry that person. Others believe that there are two, or three, or even several chances in a lifetime to find a "right enough" person for you, and that there are several right enough people if you can find them. In either case, everyone agrees that such kismet is rare.

Whichever opinion is correct, it is certain that if, among all the people on earth, spread across all the continents, you can find a right or right enough person for you during your lifetime that is a terrific feat. When you find the someone who possesses the characteristics that you seek, is geographically accessible, is also ready and available and who comes along when you are ready and available—that is *most excellent* luck.

If you were fortunate enough to meet such a person, wouldn't it be a terrible shame if the relationship didn't work out because of your patterns, or that person's patterns, or both of your patterns together? It would be a terrible romantic tragedy. But that is exactly what often happens.

I have met many people who tell a story of a broken heart. Many of them still long for that one special person with whom things didn't work out. Upon nitty-gritty investigation, we usually discover that the relationship didn't work out because of patterns.

Relationship patterns are indiscriminate. They will take over and control the course of your relationships whether you are in the right relationship for you or not. Your pattern is not going to respectfully bow out of your life and decline to mess things up just because you've found someone who is a "keeper."

Meeting Your Match

Just as disturbing is the fact that the presence of unproductive patterns can blur your ability to determine who is the right person for you. This confusion can come early and interfere with dating. Or, such confusion can come later in the relationship. I have met many people who are deeply involved with a partner, or even married to that partner, and still don't know if that person is right enough for them.

If you break your unproductive relationship pattern and begin looking at your partner with unpatterned eyes, it can actually help you discover whether or not you are with the right or wrong person. Being confused about whether the person you are with is the right person can be a sign that you are participating in a relationship pattern that is blurring your vision.

Once you are free from relationship patterns, then you are no longer playing into the negative cycle within your relationship. Once you are no longer participating in the unproductive relationship pattern, it will be easier for you to see what is really going on and it will be more possible to evaluate your partner and whether your partner is right for you.

Applying the SUBGAP method to breaking patterns in

your love life will benefit you either way. If you discover that when the patterns are removed, the love comes rushing back into your relationship, your relationship has a chance for lifelong happiness. When the blurriness from your pattern is lifted, you might discover that you are not with someone who is right for you. That discovery puts you in a better position to decide to move on and look for the right person—sooner rather than later.

Double Jeopardy

What happens when you're in a relationship in which you and your partner *both* have patterns to deal with? And what if these two sets of patterns are doubling the challenge to establishing long-lasting love and happiness?

When unproductive relationship patterns are occurring in tandem, it is like two people drowning in the ocean. When one drowning person grabs desperately on to the other, neither is saved. For both parties, there is nowhere to go but down. That is one of the reasons that failing love relationships are so terribly painful.

The solution is for one of you (probably *you*—since you are the one reading this book first) to rise above the patterns involved. That means breaking your own patterns as well as noticing your partner's pattern and rising above both. Otherwise, elements of your partner's pattern will just continue to trigger your own, in ways that get more deeply hidden as the give-and-take goes on automatic pilot.

If one of you gets into a lifeboat, the lifeboat of freedom from patterns, you are in a position to help pull the other person out of the ocean if that person so wishes to join you in the lifeboat. If neither of you gets into the lifeboat and out of the stormy sea of patterns, the chances of a happy outcome are minimized.

Two unproductive patterns can feed off each other in a fashion that intensifies both. That is why the decay caused by patterns in love relationships is often faster than that caused by patterns in other areas of life. The interlocking of hearts and minds between the two people in a relationship is a double-edged sword.

It's Not Always About You

In love relationships, it is important to see and understand not only your own unproductive patterns, but also the unproductive patterns of your partner, to have the best chance of breaking your pattern and breaking the interlocking cycle of unproductive patterns in a relationship.

As I have discussed in previous chapters, there is a freedom in understanding that some of your more bothersome thoughts, feelings, words, and actions are your pattern and *not you*. Similarly, within a relationship, there is the additional freedom of understanding that some of your partner's bothersome thoughts, feelings, words, and actions are *not about you!*

When you can remind yourself that some of what you are seeing is your partner's pattern, you don't have to take it so personally. You can say to yourself, "This is his or her pattern and *not* necessarily a reflection on me."

Without being able to determine the role of patterns in relationships, many people who feel unfulfilled in love are left asking themselves, "Is it me? Is it my partner? Or is it both of us?"

Same Pattern, Different Partner

If an unproductive relationship pattern is at the root of underfulfillment in your love life, and you change partners without breaking your pattern, you may notice a similarly unsatisfying outcome in other relationships. It is possible that you are carrying your pattern from partner to partner.

If there was never an original basis in love and tenderness in the relationship, removing patterns from the picture will not suddenly make love appear. However, if you are in the right relationship, and patterns have soured the love in your relationship over time, removing patterns from the picture could be all that is needed for the love to regrow.

So, as you can tell, there are many upsides to breaking

relationship patterns and many downsides to allowing them to continue to hurt your love life.

Under the Ginkgo Trees: A Case of Relationship Patterns

As I raise the issue of dueling relationship patterns and their souring effect on love, I am immediately reminded of Steve and Ellen, a couple that came to me when they were both quite sure their marriage was unsalvageable.

Steve was a general surgeon, Ellen an admissions officer at a college-level art school. To the outside world they looked like the perfect couple. Both were attractive, fit, witty, and very sophisticated people. And they had many interests in common. Both were well versed in art, literature, theater, and music. When things had been good between them, they had loved walking together, going to great restaurants, and sharing each other's company.

They had been madly in love and wildly attracted to each other when they met. But now, after seven years of marriage, they had reached the point where they couldn't stand each other. At the time that they came to talk with me, they were getting on each other's nerves every day. They fought constantly and hadn't had sex for two years.

Since their skirmishes occurred daily, it didn't take them long to come up with examples to examine in nitty-gritty detail.

A Stroll down Pattern Lane

The first incident they talked about was a recent stroll along a sidewalk that had taken them near a stand of ginkgo trees.

Ginkgoes, it should be said, are not the friendliest of urban trees. The female trees bear fruit heavily in the fall, and when ginkgo fruit is crushed, it emits a noxious, sulfurous smell.

The picture is this: Ellen and Steve are walking along a street in their neighborhood. They approach a section of sidewalk lined with ginkgoes, where the path ahead is littered with the fallen, rotting fruit. Before she knows it, Ellen has stepped on one of them.

According to Ellen, she was revolted that the smelly gingko fruit got on her new shoes, and when she suggested that they walk on the other side of the street, Steve responded with an outburst of fury. Ellen recalled him saying, "Do you think I *want* to walk through that muck? Of course I was going to cross the street!" Then Ellen reported that, given that she was appalled by his anger, she fought back. She told him that he didn't have to "use that tone with her!" and insisted that she "won't be spoken to in that way!" An argument ensued.

According to Steve, Ellen's "request" to cross the street was loaded with accusation. He recalled her saying, "Why do you make us walk through this smelly stuff?" He heard her insist, "If you were at all considerate, you really should walk on the other side of the street!" From Steve's point of view, Ellen had already torn into him before he had a chance to make any kind of move at all. Then, feeling he had been unjustly "tried and convicted," he fought back. An argument ensued.

Ellen felt that Steve's harsh reply was "over the top" and inconsiderate toward her. To her, it seemed obvious that they were just about to wade into the littered area of the sidewalk, where they would have been assaulted by the disgusting smell. She couldn't understand—how could he be so oblivious to how upsetting that would be to her? To Ellen, it seemed completely reasonable that she had been impatient at that moment. In her view, Steve was just "ignoring her feelings as usual."

After this discussion, I had a chance to meet with each of them individually. "So," said Ellen, "can't you see why I find it so hard to talk to him?" "Obviously," confided Steve, "you can see why I find it so hard to talk to her!"

SUBGAP Times Two

You can break unproductive patterns in a relationship by using a variation of the SUBGAP method that we have already reviewed in this book. The only added dimension is that, while trying to break your own pattern in the relationship, it is additionally helpful if you can understand the pattern in which your partner is participating.

When conditions are good, the intimacy of close relationships and marriages intensifies the rewards. But under patterned conditions, that same intimacy can have the opposite effect. Instead of helping and nurturing each other—each spouse's pattern participation intensifies the other's unproductive pattern. Pattern begets pattern. It appeared that this was what was happening with Ellen and Steve, and it became clear as each of them worked on seeing and understanding their own parts of the pattern.

Her *Pattern*

As we began to explore Ellen's contribution to the painful pattern, she came to an operational understanding of what was going on. As soon as she felt that something was going off track, she panicked. Her panic worsened if she noticed that Steve was also getting off track. She realized that she was single-mindedly focused on the feeling that *someone* had to quickly "correct" course for both of them or disaster would ensue.

Ellen gained a historical understanding of her pattern which added more clarity. She came from a very strict family. Her father, the conductor of a chamber orchestra, had a dictatorial personality. He tolerated no mistakes. When he corrected people, he made no attempt to sugarcoat his words.

Ellen recalled how, as a young adult away at college, she had written letters to her father that he returned to her . . . with grammar corrections! Needless to say, each returned and corrected letter was like a slap in the face. It took away all the pleasure of writing to him.

After developing this understanding of her own pattern, it didn't take long for Ellen to make the connection to her relationship with Steve. Let an edge come into his voice, and Ellen immediately felt "corrected," and not gently. Each correction was like a slap in the face.

But, having been the recipient of such corrections herself, she could imagine what Steve might be feeling when she corrected him—what he might have felt like in the ginkgo fruit incident.

Her historic understanding of her own pattern gave her some insight into her partner's extreme reaction and a renewed compassion—a feeling she had not had toward Steve for years.

His *Pattern*

Steve didn't know why he would "go on the defensive" as soon as he heard Ellen "complaining" or "correcting him." Upon reviewing the details of the ginkgo incident along with many others, he saw that his pattern was to react strongly whenever his wife complained about him and to get very wrapped up in defending his actions.

While further exploring such incidents, Steve noticed that he felt his judgment was on the line and called into question.

He didn't see Ellen as a panicking person who was repeating a pattern dating back to her childhood. He felt no sympathy for her plight.

Steve felt that Ellen's implication that he wasn't being considerate of her in such situations "cut him to the quick" since he viewed himself as "an officer and a gentleman" who did his best to be considerate. In reviewing the nitty-gritty details of his jumping to his own defense, Steve seemed to think it was necessary to present his entire résumé to Ellen to remind her that "other people" didn't think he was so thoughtless.

He had served as a medical officer at Nha Trang Field Hospital during the Vietnam War—hazardous, demanding work.

"No one *there* thought I was incompetent," he added. These days, he came home from a job where he spent long hours in the operating room, overseeing doctors, nurses, and staff who unquestioningly deferred to his decisions. Only at home with Ellen, it seemed, were his judgment, ability, and competency called into question.

When looking at his history, Steve reported watching his mother quietly serve his father. He remembered that, for instance, she would take the burnt piece or the smaller portion for herself, and offer the best to Steve's father. Still, her efforts always fell short in her husband's eyes and he criticized her in front of the family. Steve was furious at his father for this ungrateful behavior. When he understood his pattern, he understood that he was reacting not only on his own behalf when Ellen criticized him, but also on his mother's behalf.

As a matter of fact, he saw that he became so caught up in his reaction that he did ignore Ellen's panicked feelings during these incidents.

Their *Pattern*

While participating in her pattern, Ellen didn't notice that Steve was hurt by the implication that he was inconsiderate. In her panic, all Ellen could see was that Steve was not only ignoring her needs but was overreacting with anger "out of the blue." All she needed was some consideration right at that second. Instead she felt attacked and went into a tailspin. Of course she would accuse him of insensitivity.

While swallowed up by the feelings associated with his pattern, it never occurred to Steve that his wife needed his assistance. Steve only could focus on Ellen's questioning his judgment and ignoring his willingness to be helpful if given half a chance. He was insulted. His self-image was at stake. He felt demeaned, and thus he defended himself angrily.

So one pattern collided with another—and from that collision, the hostilities just escalated.

The Best *Aphrodisiac*

At the core, Ellen and Steve both longed for the kind of mutually respectful and considerate relationship that they once had shared, when they weren't predisposed to be at odds at the drop of a hat. When Ellen longed to be understood and have her wishes respected, and Steve longed to be counted upon as a trustworthy and competent, they were wishing to be valued by the other. But their patterns fed into a mutual relationship pattern of resentments and hurt feelings.

Admiration is an aphrodisiac, and resentment kills romance. Here was a formerly polite, considerate, romantic couple who were once very much in love, behaving daily in petty and somewhat hostile ways toward each other. As relationship patterns wear people down, the very last vestiges of civility begin to wear thin.

When you think about the ideal of love, you think about climbing the highest mountain or swimming across the widest ocean for the sake of the one you love. How is it that swimming the widest ocean once seemed worthwhile but, when partners are struggling with unproductive patterns, even a polite conversation seems too much of an effort? When patterns infiltrate into a love relationship, they take over the way a virus takes over the body. The body of the relationship starts to become ill, more sensitive to annoyances and slights.

When you are participating in patterns, you are in your own world and you can't see the big picture. Sometimes this causes you to focus on the details that are important in your pattern, to the exclusion of details that are important to your happiness, your partner's happiness, or in the health of your relationship.

If You Loved Me . . .

This seemingly elegant couple once had everything in common. They were two people who had been head over heels in love, known among their friends for dancing a scalding Argentinean tango, and would have laid down their lives for each other. Now they screamed out their venom over petty matters, such as whether one of them forgot to make hotel reservations, or who left the half-filled coffee cup alongside the sofa.

When I talked with Steve and Ellen separately, each expressed the hope that the other would "come around." Translated, this meant that each of them wanted to hold on to their own patterns in the fond (but futile) hope that the other person would "come around" and do the breaking. So, despite understanding their own and their partner's patterns, the bickering persisted as each one waited for the other to improve things first.

It was Ellen who finally said she wanted a return to the "elegant" couple they used to be, and that rang a bell with Steve. Maybe there was still a basis of love under all the trouble.

An Elegant Success

It happened on another walk, when Steve quickened the pace and Ellen found herself struggling to keep up.

At that moment, Ellen felt a situation taking place that

had to be immediately corrected. Steve, she felt, was forcing her into a situation where she could only speed up or lag behind. She'd been having trouble with her knee while on the treadmill recently, and though she hadn't complained about it, she knew if she tried to go any faster, the pace would cause it to ache. But if she lagged behind, he would just go on without her and she would be even more upset.

Ellen instantly felt like blurting out, "Why do you have to race ahead?" and "Can't you be more considerate and slow down!" or "I can't keep up with you!"

In many previous situations, that's exactly what she would have said, and from there they would have been swept into rapid-fire exchanges of defensive words and harsh recriminations.

This time, she reported that something different happened inside her head. She took a look at the things she felt like saying, and reflected to herself, "How elegant would that be?" And she answered herself, "Not very."

This time, after having seen and understood her own pattern, Steve's pattern, and their mutual relationship pattern, she was able to say something different. Fighting her impulse to panic, she said, "Steve, would you mind if we slowed down a bit? I don't feel like walking quickly today, and I'm worried about my knees."

In those few words, Ellen managed to say what she required, but without the embellishment of urgently correcting her husband. Ellen reported that she could barely constrain the impulse to lecture Steve about walking considerately. Yet contain it she did.

And then, the most amazing thing happened.

Steve said, "Of course!" He realized after having seen and understood his own pattern, Ellen's pattern, and their mutual pattern that she needed his cooperation. And then, in a patternless moment, all the resentments washed away and he felt something for Ellen that he thought was all but dead inside himself.

Steve felt warm and loving, the way he used to, and without missing a beat he took her arm, saying, *"Posso darti un braccio?"* ("Can I offer you an arm?")

Ellen thought to herself that the last time Steve had used that elegant phrase, they had been walking the streets of Rome on their honeymoon, and her own heart melted.

The love was back, and they felt it for the rest of the walk that day. It had never really gone away, but it had been over-shadowed by their patterns and patterned feelings.

Of course, as you already know by now, this one breaking success alone would not eliminate the problem. It would take numerous similar events of breaking, sometimes initiated by Ellen and sometimes by Steve, for the tide to really turn. And it would require both of them learning to guard the relationship against their pattern to keep their marriage safe.

Free to Love Again

In relationships where there was love before, and it is still there, buried underneath the patterned life, this outcome is common once patterns are broken. On the other hand, there are exceptions. For instance, where there never was love and tenderness in the relationship, removing patterns from the picture will not suddenly make love appear. Likewise, in those instances where irreversible damage has taken place in the relationship and the seeds of love are no longer alive, breaking relationship patterns will *not* grow back the love.

But for the vast majority of loving relationships where patterns have eaten away at love, the SUBGAP method offers hope. When both partners feel, deep down, that the potential for love still exists beneath the surface, then removing unproductive patterns from a relationship might just be the required love potion.

Most people really want to treat each other well, and most people feel good about themselves when they behave in a generous and compassionate way toward the one they love.

"Love is patient, love is kind" states the Bible in a quote often used in wedding ceremonies. We *all* aspire to expressing and receiving this kind of love in our relationships and marriages. Breaking free from patterns makes way for this heartfelt path.

CHAPTER 20

The Unpatterned Life

FREUD SAID THAT we have a "life instinct" and a "death instinct."

He wrote a great deal on these two subjects, and in my years of practicing psychoanalysis, I have come to understand that what he meant by this is we have *choices in how we live our lives.* By robbing you of the opportunity to fulfill your potential for success and happiness, your unproductive pattern wastes your precious time on this earth.

Isn't it about time you chose to follow your "life instinct" and break your patterns?

Freud defined the life instinct as a drive for love, enjoyment, self-preservation, creativity, and a unifying force that joins us with others. But he did not define the death instinct as strictly associated with violence and death, although those two factors were in the definition. Freud also associated the death instinct with the loss of momentum, a seeking only of the status quo, and a state where any joy of living—joie de vivre—was absent. And, as E. E. Cummings said, "The most wasted of all days is one without laughter."

If you are freed from your unproductive patterns, if your potential is unleashed, then life is much more of an adventure. You can regain a spirit of exploration, head into new and exciting territory in your life, and have more fun. Instead of expecting *more of the same* when you get up in the morning, you might just find yourself looking forward to what tomorrow will bring.

Even if you haven't had that feeling for a long time, you'll recognize it when you feel it. It comes right before you are about to do something new, something that is fun, exciting, interesting, or challenging—something that you've always wanted to do. It comes at that moment when you realize, through the successful use of the SUBGAP method, *"I'm getting to be the way I've always wanted to be!"* and *"I'm getting to live the way I've always wanted to live!"*

Joy of Living

Unproductive patterns not only reduce your happiness—they stifle the happiness you can bring to others. You have more energy to be supportive and even more capacity for love once you are no longer preoccupied with participating in your pattern. And you can be a positive influence on the people close to you when you are moving ahead in joyous, creative, life-affirming leaps and bounds.

What happens when you become more of yourself, when you come into your own? According to one of my patients, "It is like the biblical message, 'Be in the world not of the world.'" You can be into a lot of things and meet with all kinds of challenges but not be thrown off track by them if you have a good sense of yourself. When you have broken your patterns, you can stay "on purpose."

It is an adjustment to go from feeling unfulfilled with great untapped potential, to becoming fulfilled and feeling proud of yourself for living up to your potential. It may not be something to which you are accustomed at first. But, it's a happy adjustment. It is akin to winning the lottery. Whereas once you were poor and struggling, suddenly you have to adjust to more riches.

But in breaking your patterns, you gain more than money. Your winnings include accomplishment of your goals, a more satisfying career, more fulfilling relationships, a smoother and more competent way of managing your life, and higher self-esteem.

Trust me, that the joy of living is stored away inside of you somewhere. If you don't feel that way often enough, it is not because you have lost that capacity. Instead, as you've discovered in reading this book, it may simply be held in check by your patterns.

Why am I such a believer? As I have suggested at several points throughout this book, I am not just writing about something I have observed in my patients, but also something that I know from my own life. I have become who I had always imagined I *could be* but was not able to *become* until I had broken my pattern.

A Case of Unpatterned Living: The *Not-So-Mad* Doctor

I am a card-carrying member of the baby boomer generation, born in 1957. Like the fathers of most Americans my age, my father served in World War II. He fought against the Japanese in Burma. Something happened to him there, but I never found out exactly what, as he kept it secret until the day he died. Whatever occurred, one thing was certain: he never recuperated from his experiences.

As I was growing up, I gradually became aware of his scars—both physical and psychological. There was a bullet-hole-shaped scar on his back. He had an undying hatred of the Japanese. I saw bloodstained souvenirs that he had taken from enemy soldiers. Worst of all were his violent, blind rages, during which he seemed to feel he was back in the jungles of Burma—venting, usually on me, until he exhausted himself.

Looking back with the eyes of a psychoanalyst, I can easily say that my father was visited by flashbacks of his traumatic experiences in Burma. I can see now that I was simply a player in a horrifying reenactment that took place in his mind. I was the enemy and he was fighting for his life. It was nothing personal, it was just a war reenactment. But tell that to a kid.

During my father's flashbacks, I learned quickly, from trial and error, that in his madness any sound or motion on my part inspired him to think his "enemy" was still alive and a threat to him. My mother was never targeted the way I was, but that's because she had learned to hide until the episodes were over. My father never allowed me similar retreat. I learned that if I moved around, cried out, tried to escape or defend myself, my father's rampages became more furious and occasionally life-threatening. I developed a pattern of remaining stoically motionless in the face of the onslaught. To restrain any sign of upset, which would also worsen his reaction, I also became emotionally blank during the episodes.

My Rude Awakening

Using this historical perspective, I could understand a number of unproductive patterns in myself, most prominent among which was the "protective" habit of remaining sto-ically passive and unexpressive in the face of emergencies.

This pattern was to become so ingrained that it would be many years before I broke it.

A revealing incident occurred when I was in my early twenties. Out jogging one evening, I was attacked by a gang of eight to ten teenagers. Some of the gang members grabbed me and held me to the ground while others kicked me in the face and ribs. Fortunately for me there were bystanders who quickly called the police. At the first sound of sirens, the pack broke and ran, leaving me bloodied and injured on the pavement.

The next day, I reported the incident to my own psychoanalyst, Dr. Lucas. "Yeah, well, I have a few broken ribs," I told him. "When I got to the emergency room, one eye was swollen shut. I couldn't open my mouth because my jaw had been kicked out of its sockets and was dislocated, so the doctors there pulled it back into place."

"Don't you think you are being a little matter-of-fact about this?" asked Dr. Lucas.

He was right. Since I had been accustomed to suffering through brutality during my childhood, and since I was well practiced in maintaining a stoic pattern in response to attacks, my response was totally deadened.

I realized that my pattern had held me back. I could have done more in my own defense than I did. I had just started to learn martial arts, and though I was far from an expert, still, I did know some self-defense techniques. I did not use them.

With Dr. Lucas's help, I looked at the nitty-gritty details of what happened—the kind of process that I do with my patients today. I realized that, because of my pattern, I had remained more motionless than I should have under the circumstances. Without being aware, I was participating in my pattern. True, had I reacted faster and more vigorously just to defend myself, I still would have lost the fight. True, the number against me was overwhelming. But I would have felt better about my actions, and I might have avoided being so badly injured.

I Should Have, Would Have, Could Have

Upon further investigation of my life, I also started to notice that this pattern applied not only to moments where physical mobilization was required, but also to moments where mental mobilization was needed. In situations where there was no confrontation, just the need for a quick response, I had the same pattern of nonreaction. My pattern was holding me in check. And that certainly wasn't the way I *wanted* to be.

When I thought about the people whom I held up as real heroes, they were brave people who reflexively did the right thing at the right moment. I didn't admire my own hesitation in situations where a quick response was called for.

I remembered an incident that took place when I was

fourteen. Walking to school, I had witnessed an accident in which a car swerved off the road and into a light pole at high speed. A crowd gathered around the car. I watched the whole thing and just walked by without reaction.

About twenty paces later, I caught myself. I ran back to the car. Inside was one of my classmates and her mother. I asked the crowd if anyone had called an ambulance. No one had. I quickly checked that both mother and daughter were conscious and not seriously bleeding, then ran to a phone booth, called an ambulance, called my classmate's father, and ran back to the car to assist.

I did the right things. But those intervening twenty steps—the delay in reacting—really bothered me. I wasn't proud of that. As so often happened to me when my pattern was in the way, I did not react quickly to simply do what I *knew was right*.

I also realized that in many ways, the cumulative effect of these small hesitations added up to many missed opportunities.

As you probably know from experience, it is a pretty common pattern to make the wrong choice under the pressure of the moment, or make no choice at all, and to then regret it later when you look back on it. How many of us say to ourselves, "I should have done this!" or "If I only had said that!" or "If I had just kept my mouth shut!" or "If I had only said something!" In hindsight, I could always see what I *should* have done.

SUBGAP:
The Guided and Unguided Tours

I worked on my pattern in all the ways that I have described in this book. That gang attack, back in my twenties, became a turning point. It led to a dawning awareness of my unproductive pattern and—emerging from that—the desire to break it. My own psychoanalyst provided expert guidance but the "heavy lifting"—the work of seeing, understanding, breaking, and guarding against—was my own.

When people come to my office to work on breaking their patterns, they are actually doing the work themselves. They are helping themselves under my guidance and with the right tools. They are doing the heavy lifting themselves. You have seen this in the case examples. You will have to judge for yourself whether a "guided" or "unguided" tour of your pattern is right for you. The tools of the SUBGAP method can be used either way. And, in either case, the work will be *your own.*

For me, it's gratifying to know that, thanks to having broken and successfully guarded against my patterns, I have been able to move ahead when opportunities arose. As a result, it was possible for me to develop a career as a psychoanalyst, teacher, and author. When fortune placed once-in-a-lifetime chances for happiness in my path, I was now able to leap at them without hesitation.

One such leap catapulted me from Philadelphia and landed me in Seoul, South Korea, as a lecturer on psychoanalysis—so that I didn't miss the chance to continue a relationship with the woman who was later to become my wife and mother of our child. And, before we come to the end of this book, I will share with you the story of another important leap.

The Leap in My Life

Twenty years after the street gang incident drove home the point about my patterns, I received a compelling reminder of the rewards of unpatterned living.

Returning from a long trip, my wife, three-year-old daughter, and I came into the main foyer of our house, which was situated at the bottom of a long flight of stairs. Before calling it a night, I had a few things to check in my first-floor home office. My wife and daughter headed upstairs.

I had just stepped into the office when I heard my wife scream. I spun around and ran back out in time to see my daughter tumbling head over heels down the staircase. In another instant, she would have crash-landed into the hardwood landing at the foot of the stairs—a potentially catastrophic fall. Her momentum was terrific. My wife, racing down behind her, would never be able to grab her in time.

It took me only an instant to cover the twenty feet from

my office door to the foot of the stairs. I took a headlong dive, sliding into position with hands outstretched just as my daughter made her final somersault into my arms.

I made the leap, literally and figuratively!

The whole incident must have taken place in about two seconds. No hesitancy, no delay, just right action and my daughter was safe. When she zoomed into my arms, nice as you please, she said, "Daddy, you caught me like a ball!"

I suppose, to her three-year-old eyes, I made it look easy. Little did she realize what led up to it. I had traveled a long path from my father's fits, through the street gang incident, to the point where I could catch her without a millisecond of hesitancy. I *know* I would never have been able to do what I did at that moment if I hadn't done the work needed to break my pattern.

Does this mean I don't have to continue to guard against my pattern? Of course not. I still have to maintain my awareness. Once a pattern-a-holic, always one. I readily admit it. But I am not actively participating in my pattern.

I am a recovering pattern-a-holic. I am proud of it. You can be in recovery from your patterns, too. And you can be proud of yourself as well by traveling the same road, and going through all the same steps of the SUBGAP method that I have recommended to you in this book.

Without experiencing it yourself, it is impossible to completely fathom the difference between patterned and unpatterned living. As Helen Keller said, "The best and most beautiful things in the world cannot be seen or even touched. They must be felt with the heart." When you move from patterned to unpatterned living, I am confident that you too will feel this difference with your own heart.

On Your Way

When you finally come out the other side, you will agree that the unpatterned life is a miraculous thing. Even people who used to say, "I don't think I could be any other way" or "I am not hardwired for that" or "It's not my fate," discover that life is dramatically more vibrant and fulfilling once they have broken through their unproductive patterns.

Armed with the knowledge you have gained from this book, you have a new perspective—a scientific way of looking at your own life. The tools of the SUBGAP method provide you with a step-by-step way to *see, understand, break,* and *guard against patterns.*

You can now make the leap—a leap into the life that you always sensed, deep down, would fulfill your potential.

You can sense if you have unfulfilled potential inside you. If you do, you know in your heart that the message of this book is true—*the most important thing you can do for yourself and for those you love is to make the leap and break the patterns that hold you back.*

Acknowledgments

⁓

THIS BOOK WAS made possible by the people who inspired me to navigate a path from seeker, to student, to practitioner, and finally to teacher and author.

I owe the direction of my life to the shining and dignified example set for me by my grandfather, pharmacist, and neighborhood "doctor" Ben Marks. I owe my fulfilling career to the endlessly patient and generous mentoring of my training psychoanalyst, Dr. Gerald Lucas, who showed me that it is possible to be a scientist, a fine doctor, a family man, and a compassionate being all rolled into one.

I owe my resolve and motivation in completing this book, despite a constantly overflowing patient schedule, to the unyielding love and faith of Misoon Ghim Silverberg, my wife, an extraordinary opera singer and my most ardent editor. And, I owe my never-ending excitement about seeing what the next day will bring to my daughter, Hannah Silverberg, who reminds me daily about what is *truly* important in life.

I owe my absolute confidence in presenting the ideas in this book to all of my patients who demonstrated—through their own courageous work in my office and dedicated homework in their lives—that patterns can be broken and potentials can be fulfilled.

I also owe debts of gratitude to Jin-Gap Jang, whose gentle spirit honored our household, to Yong-Je Kim for his unwavering trust, and to Alan Aarons for his good will throughout this writing and before.

It is quite clear to me that the birth of every book requires substantial publishing midwifery. Certainly, this book would not have come to be without the outspoken advocacy of my agent, Laura Gross. Nor would its message be so powerful without the comments of Janet Ruth Falon, the steadfast attention to detail of Anne Dubuisson Anderson, the "user-friendly" eye of Edward Claflin, and the good sense of Dr. Michael Bopp. I also want to acknowledge the kind assistance of Alex Alterman, Mark Hinrichs, Peter Haslanger, Jeff Byce, Elaine Terranova, Andi Buchanan, Elaine English, and Harry Rosenthal. And thanks also to Bob Savar for his help with *www.theleapbook.com*.

In the end, the clarity of my message is the direct result of the focused and invaluably thought-provoking dialogue with my editor and publisher, Matthew Lore, to whom I owe a great debt of gratitude. It is his foresight in taking a chance on a heretofore little-known psychoanalyst that puts this guidebook in your hands today.

1-669-243-6286

1-916-628-9709

816 995-3221